PSYCHOLOGICAL ISSUES

VOL. VIII, No. 1 MONOGRAPH 29

SIMILARITY IN VISUALLY PERCEIVED FORMS

by

ERICH GOLDMEIER

Foreword by IRVIN ROCK

INTERNATIONAL UNIVERSITIES PRESS, INC.
239 Park Avenue South • New York, N.Y. 10003

Library of Congress Catalog Card Number: 7[illegible]
ISBN: 0-8236-6077-X

PSYCHOLOGICAL ISSUES

Subscription per Volume, $15.00
Single Copies of This Number, $5.00

CONTENTS

PREFACE

The first six chapters of this monograph originally appeared in *Psychologische Forschung* (Goldmeier, 1936). Professor Irvin Rock became interested in the paper and it was at his initiative that this English version has come to be published. I have translated it with a minimum of change.

Since 1936, surprisingly little work has been done on similarity, even though it continues to be a basic concept in psychological theories. The newer work consists mainly of a paper by Attneave (1950), and investigations initiated by Shepard (1963) and taken up by others, that deal with various aspects of similarity space. Recently I too have done further experimental work in this area, included here as Chapter 7. The material in Chapter 7 will be drawn upon in a forthcoming paper on memory changes.

Even though this monograph is 36 years old, I hope the reader will not find it dated. The old as well as the new part deals with facets of the topic hardly touched on by others. This work will also furnish an addition to the all too small number of experimental—as opposed to theoretical—papers on Gestalt theory available in English.[1] Finally, with the advent of computers and the frustrating efforts to teach pattern recognition to these machines, an account of what might be termed human pattern processing seems even more timely now than when this essay was written.

There is a more basic reason for investigating similarity. Beginning with the earliest writings in Gestalt theory (Wertheimer, 1912b) perceptual organization has been viewed as a *field process.* Hence perceptual organization can ultimately be understood only in terms of concepts applicable to fields. Such concepts are highly developed in physics, in the form of so-called variational prin-

[1] It is planned to make available for classroom use a set of slides of some of the figures.

ciples (see, for instance, Yourgrau and Mandelstam, 1968). There is a close parallel between the thinking underlying variation in dynamics (see Lanczos, 1966) and in visual perception, between the configuration space of dynamics and the similarity space in perception, and between virtual or actual displacements in configuration space and possible or actual variation of a pattern in similarity space. In dynamics, a small variation can give rise to a restoring force. In perception, a varied pattern can tend to change toward the original one. In both cases different degrees and directions of variation enable the experimenter to test the field strength around the point of departure, the strength of the potential in dynamics, the strength of some aspect of organization of the tested pattern in pattern perception. The similarity between variants of a pattern discloses the sensitivity to change of the feature varied, reveals singularities and regions of indifference to a particular variation. Similarity experiments indicate which geometric relationships are "phenomenally real," i.e., are perceived, are characteristics of the percept, and which geometric relationships are not apprehended, are irrelevant, not "phenomenally realized." The phenomenal reality of a feature has consequences beyond similarity, e.g., for pattern memory (Goldmeier, in preparation).

In connection with the research presented in Chapter 7, I wish to thank Dr. D. V. Cicchetti of the Veterans Administration's Eastern Research Support Center, who did all the statistics, and Miss K. D. Morris, then Chief of Nursing Education, for making student nurses available as subjects for these experiments, as well as the many other employees of the Veterans Administration Hospital, Montrose, New York, who volunteered as subjects and helped in other ways. It is also a pleasure to acknowledge the contribution of Mrs. Gloria Spevacek of the Medical Illustration Service of the Veterans Administration Hospital, Bronx, New York, who prepared many experimental designs and all the illustrations in this chapter.

E. G.

FOREWORD

IRVIN ROCK

Among the many classic experiments we repeated as part of our training in experimental psychology at the New School for Social Research were those of Zeigarnik, Ovsiankina, Gottschaldt, and Goldmeier. Goldmeier's experiment was on the perception of similarity, and the article was in German, published in the *Psychologische Forschung* in 1936. Like the others, no complicated apparatus was needed for the experiment, just figures drawn on cardboard. No one knew anything about Goldmeier—except that he was one of the many gifted students of the Gestalt group of psychologists—or what had become of him, whether he had survived Hitler and the war.

Imagine my surprise, therefore, when one day not too long ago a distinguished-looking gentleman introduced himself at a symposium on psychology in New York as Erich Goldmeier. He had come to the United States in 1938 and had been practicing medicine, while also keeping up with developments in psychology. He, of course, had no idea that his name and his paper on similarity were well-known to a small group of us who had received our training at the New School. Out of this meeting came the idea of making his article on similarity available to English-speaking psychologists, since it is clear that at present this work is known in America and elsewhere to only a very few.

The contrast between Goldmeier's research of 1936 and much of contemporary experimental work in America is illuminating. Goldmeier starts with a problem in psychology and proceeds to search for laws or principles that will make sense of the facts. He does *not* approach the problem by immediately seeking *quantita-*

tive relationships (in this case between change of physical attributes and judgments of similarity), recognizing that such an endeavor must await clarification of more fundamental questions. Nor does he immediately search for answers in neurophysiology, information theory, computer analogues, or mathematical models. Contemporary psychologists more and more tend to seek explanations not *within* psychology, but outside of it, in neighboring disciplines that at the moment are enjoying great prestige. It is as if they do not consider mental facts to be real. All too often this tendency results in a failure to advance our knowledge of the psychological problem under investigation. One might say that psychology has become one of the most sophisticated and one of the most sterile of disciplines. In contrast, Goldmeier's research is imaginative and penetrating. His method is simplicity itself. Observers are asked to indicate which of two comparison figures appears to be more similar to a standard figure. The figures are designed to test a particular hypothesis about similarity. No high-powered statistics are employed; indeed no statistics at all are needed, as a rule, because the outcome is usually crystal clear. Yet this monograph tells us more about similarity in form perception than any other work before or since. It is an outstanding example of the thinking and experimentation that Wertheimer and the early Gestalt movement inspired.

Similarity has always been a topic of central interest to psychologists but, with few exceptions, similarity itself has not been the problem under study. One of the few areas of research which can be said to have focused on the problem of similarity was that of stimulus equivalence. Köhler, Lashley, and Klüver sought to find out what patterns were similar to others by first training an animal on a discrimination problem and then substituting new patterns. If the animal continued to show a strong preference, then the preferred pattern was presumably perceived as similar (or identical) to the one for which it was substituted. These investigators all concluded that preservation of figural *relationships* was the crucial factor for equivalence.

But generally some other phenomenon has been of central interest—and similarity has been considered to be a relevant determinant of that phenomenon. Similarity is assumed to be a major determinant of stimulus generalization, associative learn ing, transfer of training, and forgetting. It is also implicated in perceptual grouping, form perception, and recognition. As far as stimulus generalization is concerned, most of the work done has used a stimulus parameter that varies along a continuum specifiable in physical terms, such as wave length, intensity, and the like. Of course, by and large, two stimuli are experienced as more similar the closer they are to one another in their physical properties, and generalization gradients reflect this fact. Obvious as the *fact* may be, however, we have no full explanation of why phenomenal similarity does closely correspond to degree of similarity of physical attributes. It is reasonable to suppose that there is a good deal that is common to the neural events underlying sensory experiences that are similar. Thus, for example, both red and orange colors will stimulate retinal cone cells that are primarily sensitive to longer wave lengths of light. But difficult problems arise. Tones an octave apart are experienced as more similar than those whose frequencies are more nearly the same; violet and red seem similar although they result from wave lengths at opposite ends of the visible spectrum. The "solution" has been to define similarity operationally in terms of stimuli that yield the maximum generalization in behavior. But this is of course completely circular, since generalization was originally defined in terms of similarity. If we follow this prescription, we can never predict generalization. It leaves us with no theory of generalization and no understanding of similarity.

Goldmeier does not address his inquiry to this problem of similarity of sensations corresponding to physical energy continua, referring to it with Stumpf's term, "similarity of the simple." His decision to concentrate on the problem of similarity among complex objects is based on the belief that complex percepts can be analyzed whereas simple sensations cannot. If true, it would seem to follow that no further psychological clarification of "similarity of the simple" is to be expected and that the explanation will therefore necessarily be neurophysiological, whereas there may be much in the way of nonphysiological explication that can be given in the case of "similarity of the complex" before the ultimate statement about underlying brain events.

Occasionally, when human subjects were employed in studies of stimulus generalization, more complex aspects of the stimulus were varied, such as the shape of the nonsense figure. Similarity was then manipulated on the basis of intuition rather than on the basis of any principles. Typically, judges rated figures for degree of similarity before the experiment was carried out. Generalization was, of course, found to be a function of similarity as thus defined, but obviously this procedure sheds little light on the determinants of similarity.

The work on learning, transfer, and forgetting has been predicated on the assumption that learning is impeded and transfer is negative where the stimuli in the associations to be learned are similar (the responses being different) and interference, causing forgetting, is maximum. Thus stimulus generalization as initially studied in animal conditioning was assumed to be operating in human associative learning and recall. If the stimuli in a paired-associate list were similar to each other or similar to stimuli in a second list, then such stimuli tended to elicit wrong responses either from within the list or from the other list, and this, of course, was an interference. More often than not the stimuli were nonsense syllables and similarity was manipulated either on the assumption that all nonsense syllables are similar, or on identity—i.e., the stimulus remained the same. I need hardly add that all of this work added little to our understanding of similarity.

Only in the area of form perception and pattern recognition has research been relevant to the problem of *what constitutes similarity.* Hebb sought to explain the fact that forms transposed in size or position are easily recognized, in terms of common parts of figures, such as lines and angles, and the integration of such parts into larger units by a sequence of eye movements. The sensory physiologists discovered cells of the visual system that respond to certain invariant features of the proximal stimulus such as curvature and orientation of edges. Computer models of pattern recognition were evolved to deal with the facts of transposition and recognition of patterns such as letters despite considerable variation from instance to instance. Some of the models stress the idea of a template, a matching of the stimulus to a prior trace of a similar stimulus, while other models—taken more seriously by psychologists—stress analysis of the pattern into its distinctive features. Selfridge, Neisser, and E. Gibson, among others, have developed theories of form perception in which such feature analysis plays a crucial role. Presumably forms are similar if they contain many features in common.

It is interesting that the theme of much of this work is the search for relevant *elements or parts,* the concatenation of which will explain the perception of the whole: cell assemblies, convexity and orientation detectors, feature analyzers. True, the elements are not punctate retinal stimuli as in the pre-Gestalt days, and often they are described relationally, but elements they are nonetheless. Now I would agree that although forms as whole qualities may be *phenomenally* indivisible, if we are to go beyond phenomenology, we must explain the basis of such wholes. Clearly this entails the parts in relation to one another. A triangle does contain three lines and three angles.[1] But what is crucial is the geometrical relationship of these parts; *it is the way they fit together* that is the essence of triangularity. Otherwise Figure Aa below would look as much like a triangle as Ab, since

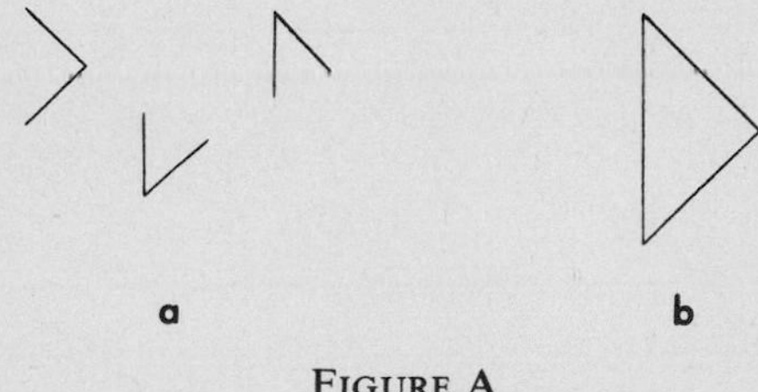

FIGURE A

both contain three angles and all the line components that make up a triangle. According to E. Gibson, what makes certain letters of the alphabet similar (and therefore highly confusable to children) is the number of distinctive features they share. For example, the letters *B* and *D* have three features in common, namely, symmetry, closed curves, and a vertical line component. But if one were to design figures taking into account these features and others the two letters do not share, would we end up with a *B* or

[1] But even this statement need not be true. A triangle can be constructed of dots rather than of lines; even of only three dots at the "corners." In that case, there are no lines and no angles as parts. These "parts" exist only after the whole has been mentally constructed, so to speak.

a *D*? For example, Figure Ba below contains all three features specified for a *D* and Bb contains all five features specified for a *B*

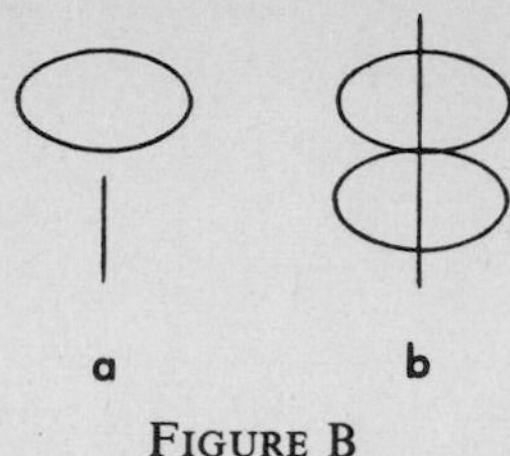

FIGURE B

(the three mentioned, plus intersection of line components and cyclic change). Thus, as far as all these approaches are concerned, Goldmeier's critique of the theory of identical elements (his Hypothesis I) is just as relevant today as it was in 1936.

Even the work on pattern recognition, though relevant, does not constitute a *direct* investigation of the problem of similarity. We infer what is similar from what is recognized. Yet recognition can imply either an impression of identity with a previously seen object or an impression of similarity. Recognition per se is not, therefore, as sensitive an index of similarity as might be desired. A further complication is that many investigators have taken identification as the index of form perception, i.e., the classification of the pattern into the correct categories (such as the letter *A*). Clearly identification entails more than perception, since the first time a pattern is encountered it is perceived but not identified. This amalgamation of identification with perception necessarily confounds the problem. Goldmeier studies the problem of similarity *directly* by asking his observers to indicate which of the alternatives is more similar to the standard figure.

What, then, does determine the degree of similarity of one figure to another? Goldmeier first shows the limitations of a theory of identical elements. Granted that forms are "whole qualities," the question then becomes: What makes one whole quality like another? The transposability of forms in size or location suggests that what is crucial are the angular and distance *relationships* within a figure or, in short, the geometry of the figure (just as the transposability of melodies suggests that what is crucial is not the sum of tones that make it up but the *relation-*

ship of intervals between tones with regard to both pitch and rhythm).

In this monograph, Goldmeier soon arrives at this hypothesis on the basis of simple experiments, but he goes on to demonstrate that it is far from a sufficient hypothesis. How would it account for the fact that Figure 12a (see below) looks more like c than like b? Figures b and c are both geometrical alterations of a and of about the same magnitude. That is, both b and c alter certain geometrical relations of a so that from a strictly mathematical or objective point of view the hypothesis does not enable us to predict the outcome. How would we account for the fact that of the two variations in Figure 11 (see below), c is clearly more similar to a? The degree of geometrical alteration is certainly greater in c than in b.

One can account for these results with certain supplementary principles. In the case of Figure 12, it would seem that the two lines within the open rectangle are seen as a pair because they are similar and near to one another. In 12c this organization is preserved whereas in b it is destroyed. It is a matter of grouping. In the case of Figure 11, it is clear that it is not the angles in c that are located physically in corresponding places that are taken to be homologous with angles in a. Homologous parts are determined by their function within the whole figure, not necessarily by what is geometrically equivalent. Figure 11a contains a central line tilted away from the sides and so does c; b has a central line parallel to the sides.

But this is still not the whole story. Why is Figure 15a (see below) more like b than like c if (1) c is actually a proportional enlargement of a whereas b is not, and if (2) both b and c preserve the grouping impression of a, namely, equally spaced dots? Goldmeier suggests that one must distinguish the form of a figure from the material of which it is constituted. He concludes that, in transposition, the impression of similarity is ordinarily best preserved by leaving the material absolutely the same, i.e., by not transposing it.[2]

[2] It is interesting to note that sophisticated computer models of pattern recognition try to allow for the fact that forms will often remain unchanged despite transpositions of size, orientation, and the like. Goldmeier's demonstrations that often similarity is *not* predictable merely on the basis of equivalence of proportions then becomes an embarrassment to these models. They explain too much.

Then there is the matter of *Prägnanz.* Some features of a figure are more important for the over-all impression than others, so that even slight changes of these features have a marked effect on similarity. Other non*prägnant* features can be substantially changed without affecting the over-all impression. Symmetry is one such *prägnant* feature, particularly if the figure is symmetrical about its vertical axis. For example, in Figure 54 (see below), c looks more like a than does b because it is symmetrical about its vertical axis but not about its horizontal axis (a is symmetrical about both axes); the converse is true of b. The result is that in both a and c, symmetry is *realized* phenomenally (to use a term emphasized by Goldmeier) whereas in b it is not, although objectively speaking it is just as symmetrical as is c. There are other *prägnant* features the alteration of which markedly influences similarity, such as parallelity, horizontality, and other types of regularity.

Ordinarily the concept of *Prägnanz* is one of the weak links in the Gestalt theory, because it is either vaguely defined or empirically unproven. It presumably means the tendency to perceive patterns in the simplest, most regular, or most symmetrical manner possible, i.e., there is a preference for organizations that are optimally simple. [3] However that may be, the term *Prägnanz* has also been used with a slightly different shade of meaning, one that is perfectly clear. By *prägnant,* Goldmeier means a "singular," or special, value of a parameter. For example, a straight line can vary in its orientation, but the horizontal and vertical orientations are singular: change them even a few degrees and you make a very noticeable change. But change a line tilted 10° from the vertical to 15° from the vertical and the change may not even be noticed.

An entire chapter is devoted to the effect on similarity of change of orientation of a figure. This is an area in which I myself have done a good deal of research. I read this chapter in the original German many years ago and, of course, forgot most of it. On rereading it now—after 15 years of work on the problem—I am deeply impressed by Goldmeier's insights and demonstra-

[3] Hochberg and Attneave have attempted to reformulate the concept of *Prägnanz* in terms of information theory. The perceptual preference is for the alternative that requires the least information to describe.

tions. For example, he shows that it is not necessarily the case that the greater the disorientation of a figure, the greater the change in its appearance. It all depends on the figure and on how singular *(prägnant)* features are affected by the disorientation. (In contrast, there have been several investigations of the effect of degree of disorientation on form perception in which the methodology was perhaps rigorous but which contained little in the way of theoretical analysis and gave quantitative results that were hard to interpret.) In Figure 53 (see below), the right angles in the square a are immediately perceived as right angles because their sides are horizontal and vertical; c looks quite different because it is immediately perceived that its angles are not right angles. Figure 53d shows a tilted by 45°; here the presence of right angles is no longer perceived, and that is surely part of the reason why it looks different from a. Figure 53f (c rotated 45°) does not look so different from d because the angles in d that are altered in f are not singular. Note that the physical difference between pair d-f is the same as that between a-c.

In one of his experiments, Goldmeier anticipated a finding that was fully established only some years later, namely, that it is not the changed orientation of its retinal image but rather the changed *phenomenal* orientation of a figure that produces the profound difference in the way it looks. This can be demonstrated by presenting the figure in a new orientation and requiring the observer also to assume this new orientation. For example, if Figure 53a is rotated until it is in the position of d it looks like a diamond, and it continues to look like a diamond when viewed with head tilted 45°. Yet the image of the figure is now again "a square." The observer assumes that the top of the figure is the region that is uppermost in the environment, that is, he is not "taking" the same region to be the top as he did before it was tilted. It is this change in what is seen as top, bottom, and sides that accounts for the change in the figure's appearance. Or, to cite another example, the impression of symmetry based on equality of the sides of a figure with respect to a vertical axis is preserved even if the observer views the figure with head tilted 45°; the impression of symmetry is not preserved if the figure is then tilted 45° even though the axis of symmetry of the figure is now "vertical" within the retinal image. In this case, therefore, what matters is the direction of the figure that is perceived as vertical.

Explanations based on retinal or cortical *anistropy* are ruled out because the change of retinal-cortical orientation has no effect on phenomenal appearance. The only answer I have been able to supply to the question why this altered psychological assignment of directions so profoundly affects phenomenal shape is that the figure is, cognitively speaking, a very different thing in its two orientations. Thus, Figure 51b is an irregular quadrilateral resting solidly on a base; 51f (which is b tilted 34° clockwise) is a symmetrical, diamond-shaped figure resting on a point. Something very like these two descriptions, albeit nonverbal descriptions, therefore, must determine our spontaneous impression of the figure. This conclusion is implicit in Goldmeier's analysis of the effect of change in orientation, although he did not have the evidence to enable him to know that it was not the altered orientation of the retinal image per se that was crucial.

On the basis of these and other considerations, Goldmeier ends up with the idea that similarity depends upon the phenomenal picture to which a configuration gives rise. By this he means a phenomenal impression that takes into account the geometry based on figural relationships, but also takes into account salient features such as symmetry, grouping effects such as which parts are more intimately linked to one another and which are not, and so forth. If two figures produce similar phenomenal pictures, they will appear similar. It seems clear that in this formulation Goldmeier wants to emphasize what he has demonstrated throughout, namely, that similarity is a function of mental transformations and organizations, not of the physical properties of the stimulus pattern per se. But still, to put it this way is circular. One can sympathize with him here because what he is trying to do is to incorporate all his findings under one single principle. Few psychologists have been able to do that in any area of research. In order to avoid circularity, however, it would seem necessary at this point to make statements that are not merely phenomenological descriptions. Many of his separate hypotheses are of this sort, such as those referring to grouping, form versus material, and *Prägnanz,* but when it comes to unifying all of them, some higher-level mechanism or hypothetical schema is required. A model of brain events such as the Gestalt field theory would be one possible answer, but Goldmeier steers clear of physiological theories. Besides, it is doubtful if Köhler's theory of brain action can do justice to any of the principles Goldmeier uncovers. As far as I can determine, there is no specific statement anywhere in the Gestalt literature about the nature of the brain event that is isomorphic with a perceived form or a melody. One might say that Gestalt theory has no specific theory of Gestalten. Yet one must bear in mind that the Gestalt theory I am here criticizing from the standpoint of explanatory mechanisms is the same theory that inspired Goldmeier's study and which produced the valuable descriptive formulations he puts to such good use.

A possible general solution to the problem of similarity is at least implicit in Goldmeier's analysis of the effects of changed orientation, namely, that form perception is based on a cognitive type of process. One might think of this cognition as relational in nature, but it also refers to unique aspects such as symmetry, grouping, and the like. Needless to say, it is not a process of verbal description. Rather, it is to be thought of as a hypothetical cognitive event intervening between stimulation and phenomenal experience. But here I am putting words in Goldmeier's mouth and indulging in my own speculations.

It is a commentary on psychology over the last half century that so many of the creative contributions that came out of Gestalt thinking have never been followed up. One may hope that the publication of this translation will prevent that same fate from befalling this important contribution to our knowledge of similarity.

INTRODUCTION

1. THE PROBLEM

We are often struck by the similarity between objects such as pictures or people or figures, even though we cannot conceptualize this impression. Typically, the impression is so compelling that it could be taken for an elementary mental function which serves as a basis for higher functions. As a category, similarity has been particularly important in the theory of knowledge, functioning as an ordering principle which was assumed to create units and set boundaries.

But before inquiring into the use of this concept it is necessary to investigate its meaning. So far, in spite of the intrinsic and historical importance of the concept, experiments aimed at clarifying its basic nature have been carried out only sporadically. There has been, however, an abundance of theoretical statements, usually based on the idea that almost any two complex entities which have some similarity to each other have some identical attributes along with some differing ones. But the real problem consists in determining what attributes are relevant for similarity. Everything has *some* properties in common with everything else, but only certain entities are similar to one another. It was soon recognized that not all properties–in the most general possible meaning of the word–contribute to the impression of similarity. Among Aristotle's definitions *(Metaphysics,* Vol. 9, 1018a, 15f.) is the case, among others, of one item being similar to another if it has in common with it "the most *or the most important* extremes within which it may vary." The entire subsequent history of this problem appears as an attempt to determine which these "most important" attributes are that lead to the impression of similarity, an attempt which was complemented by efforts directed toward the elusive goal of finding a simple and mathematically precise formula for it.

In addition to the similarity of complex entities mentioned so far, there is also a "similarity of the simple" (Stumpf). Consider three musical sounds—say the musical notes c, d, and e. If the second of these is more similar to the first than is the third, it is not possible to explain this similarity by identity of *any attributes,* as has been shown conclusively by Stumpf (1883, pp. 115f.). In cases of similarity of the simple the question which are "essential" attributes has no meaning. This topic will not be considered here; the investigation will be restricted to the similarity of complex entities. It should be noted, however, that phenomenally there is no basic difference between the similarity of the simple and the similarity of complex entities. In both cases similarity is experienced directly. The reason for the similarity is not given in the naïve experience of similarity of either complex or simple entities. When it is strong enough it has a compelling character which does not appear to be accessible to introspective analysis. Especially in the case of very complex structures, faces for example, introspective reflection usually does not lead to elaboration or more basic reasons for the impression of similarity (Höffding, 1901, pp. 215f.).

It is impossible to deal in detail with the numerous opinions of earlier authors. The differences among the many formulations that have been proposed arise mainly from differing philosophical positions and cannot be discussed outside of that context. Furthermore, almost none of these propositions were tested experimentally. An exception is Mach's experiments on the effect of symmetry, which will be discussed in Chapter 6. Instead, we have arranged possible and proposed solutions in categories. As these are taken up, some of the formulations will be further discussed.

2. EXPERIMENTAL PROCEDURE

A naïve observer "sees" similarity but cannot adequately explain the basis of this impression. To obtain such information experimentally, a test object or standard must be presented with two or more other objects for comparison, and the subject asked to rank the comparison objects for their degree of similarity to the original. In this way one obtains a measure of the relative degree of similarity within the constellation examined. This rank order can then serve as the starting point for conclusions about the basis for the impression of similarity.

The following experimental procedure was used in all but a few instances, which will be specifically described. The observer (O) was shown three drawings, a standard (St) and two comparison figures (CF), and instructed to tell which comparison figure seemed to him more similar to the standard. He stood or sat in front of a table; the three drawings were presented simultaneously, the standard above and the two comparison figures side by side below it. The positions of the comparison figures were alternated from subject to subject. Every effort was made to avoid singling out one of the two comparison figures in any way whatever. The above-mentioned instruction was the only one given and was not explained further. Before the subject had time to ask for explanations he was given a practice test, usually Figure 41, which was not included in the results, with a remark such as: "You will immediately see what I mean. Which of these two pictures seems to you to be more similar to this one?" If he nevertheless asked questions the same instructions were rephrased, the suggestion of any particular criterion for the answer being carefully avoided. The drawings ranged in size from about 3″ to 8″. They were drawn in India ink on white cards large enough to allow adequate margins.

Because a large number of experiments was necessary, 10 to 20 experiments were usually combined into a series and presented to a subject one after another. The experiments combined into a series were chosen so as to avoid the establishment of a set from the earlier to the later items in a series: e.g., Figures 6 and 10, or 5 and 7, would not be given together. In a few experiments the component figures were presented successively: the standard first, then one comparison figure, and then the second comparison figure. The subject then had to "keep the figures in mind." The results were the same as when the figures were presented simultaneously; however, the decision was clearly more difficult and more tiring. The main experiments were therefore carried out with the more convenient simultaneous presentation, and only those in which the design was rotated were presented successively (see Chapter 6).

Of about 100 subjects used, all but six were unfamiliar with psychological experiments. They came from the most diverse occupations and backgrounds. Most were between 20 and 30 years old; the youngest was six years old and the oldest was over 60. There was no evidence that these differences had any particular effect. Personality differences likewise seemed to be unimportant, although one can assume that the most various types were represented among our subjects, and a conscious effort was made to avoid bias in the selection of subjects. In experiments such as these it is not expected that personality differences will matter very much, since one tries to make designs and experimental conditions as unambiguous as possible in order to make the experiment decisive.

It could be objected that this procedure investigates a situation far removed from everyday life, and that spontaneous experiences of similarity, such as with faces, may be something entirely different. It is my impression that the subjects saw these experimental tasks as no different from tasks occasionally undertaken spontaneously. But be that as it may, in theoretical discussions in which similarity functions as a category, it is applied to an almost unlimited range of objects and situations (see, for instance, Hume, *Treatise of Human Nature,* I, 1; 4 and 5). Even if the spontaneous experience of similarity between, say, faces should differ from the experience of similarity between figures in a comparison experiment, the process examined here still has the same theoretical interest. Furthermore, the procedure employed has two advantages. First, the objects used are well-defined stimuli, easily subjected to controlled variations; second, they are relatively free from uncontrolled and unpredictable experiences and biases of individual subjects, something which could not be assumed with any certainty, for instance, of faces.

Another, more subtle, objection should be discussed here. Our procedure appears to make the tacit assumption that the degree of similarity is subject to the finest gradations imaginable. It should, therefore, be possible to rank degrees of similarity in a series just as degrees of temperature or numbers can be ranked.

That is not the case, however. Psychologically there are not, for instance, arbitrarily *small* degrees of similarity. Rather, with decreasing similarity the absolute impression of "dissimilarity" eventually arises, somewhat as, with physically increasing temperatures, *psychologically* an object may eventually appear as absolutely "too hot."

Even within the range of similarity, degrees of similarity acquire qualitative differences. A high degree of similarity conveys an impression like "the same again, almost the same"; little similarity appears as "just barely related," or, finally, as "something entirely different, dissimilar"; in between there are steps like "the same in a different material," "the same in principle," and so on.

A stepwise change in quality, rather than a smooth gradation, is a property of many series, not at all limited to such classical and well-known examples as the changes of the various colors (versus the continuous scale of wavelengths). Interesting examples are found in the great variety of qualitative steps within the number series which Wertheimer (1912a) found in the number concepts of primitive peoples and also in the daily lives of civilized ones.

It is certainly much too intellectualistic to interpret our experimental figures as examples of progressive subtraction of "absolute degrees of similarity." In experimental Figure 39 (see below), for example, it would be quite artificial to say that 39c has a certain degree of similarity to the St and 39b another, lesser degree of similarity to the St. Rather, 39c is "the same done a little differently," whereas 39b is "a distortion of the original figure."

This sketch of a phenomenology of the experience of similarity, which will be enough for present purposes, demonstrates how a *certain rank order* among different steps of similarity can result just as if there existed a homogeneous, continuous scale of similarity. Actually, the steplike structure of the decrements of similarity did not lead to experimental difficulties. In general the subjects were able to perform the tasks required of them.

1

SIMILARITY AS PARTIAL IDENTITY: HYPOTHESIS I

3. VARIATION BY SUBTRACTION OR ADDITION

The theories proposed so far for the nature of similarity can be placed in a few categories, which will be discussed systematically without regard for their historical relationships.

The first attempt at explanation to be considered here sees the essential determinant of similarity in the identical occurrence of discrete parts in the two objects. It is easy to state this proposition in quantitative terms, as follows: the degree of similarity of two objects corresponds to the *number of identical parts.* Cases which seem to confirm this proposition are shown in experimental Figures 1, 2, and 3. In Figure 1, the St, la, is a triangle made

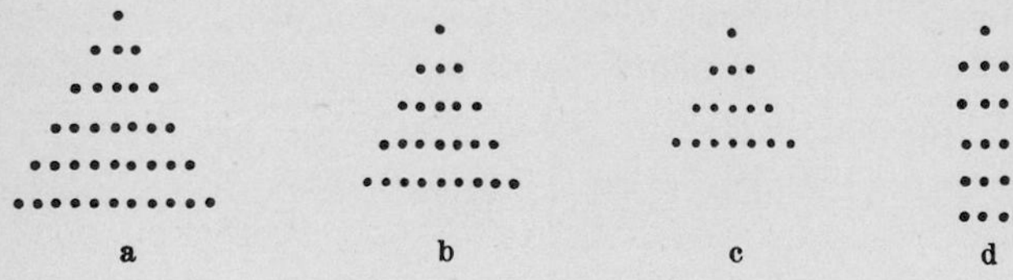

FIGURE 1

up of dots. In the CFs, 1b and 1c, some parts, i.e., dots, have been removed, more dots having been removed in 1c than in 1b. Corresponding to the number of remaining identical parts, $a \sim b \nsim c$ [1] for 7 of 8 Os. In Figure 2b and d, new parts have been added to the St, 2a: specifically, the lines in 2d are increased

[1] This combination of symbols signifies: a is more similar to b than it is to c; or, b is more similar to a than is c.

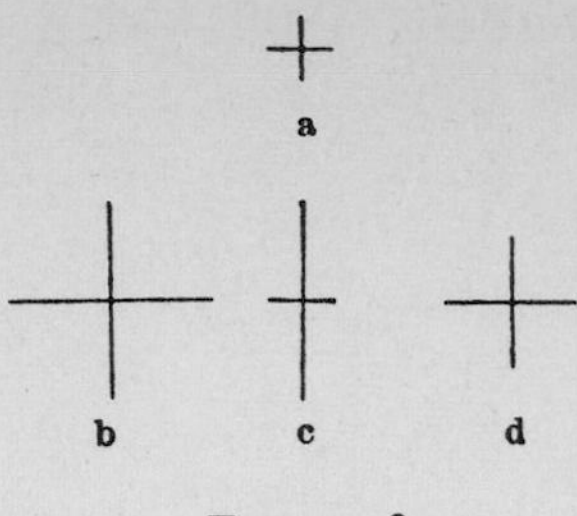

FIGURE 2

less than those in 2b. Correspondingly, the experiment results in 2a $\sim$ d $\nsim$ b for 9 of 10 Os. Similarly, in Figure 3b the short rays of 3a have been lengthened, and in 3c the same rays have been

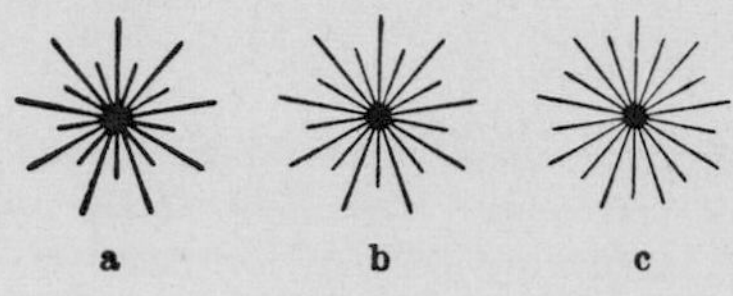

FIGURE 3

lengthened still more. The experiment results in a $\sim$ b $\nsim$ c for 10 of 10 Os. While it is obvious that in Figure 1 some "parts" have been subtracted, it may be questioned whether in Figures 2 and 3 there has been an addition of "parts" in the same sense. Figures 2b and d, for instance, can also be described as being formed from only two lines–"parts"–just like 2a, the difference between them and 2a being merely one of length. If this is to be considered an addition of new parts, it is not an addition of "natural parts" but only an addition of arbitrarily tacked-on pieces.

The variations in Figure 28 (see below) are the same kind of "addition of new parts." In this case the sizes of the dots have been varied; in CF 28b the larger dots of the St have been further enlarged, and in 28c all the dots have been enlarged. The latter CF is less similar.

The solution suggested by these experiments agrees with a frequently expressed opinion. "Similarity is partial identity," as Mach (1902) put it. A very precise formulation is found in Clauberg and Dubislav (1923, p. 14): "Objects are called 'similar' if they are equal with regard to parts." Similar definitions have been made by Münsterberg (1900, Vol. 1, pp. 553f.) and many other psychologists and logicians (see, for instance, the selection of definitions of similarity in Eisler, 1927).

4. VARIATION BY CHANGES OF PARTS

These experiments suggest that similarity depends on the number of identical, arbitrarily singled out pieces (arbitrary in the sense that these pieces are not necessarily delimited by intrinsic structural boundaries of true phenomenal parts of the pattern). The variations consisted in *addition* or *subtraction* of parts. But this is not the only possibility under Hypothesis I. Variation

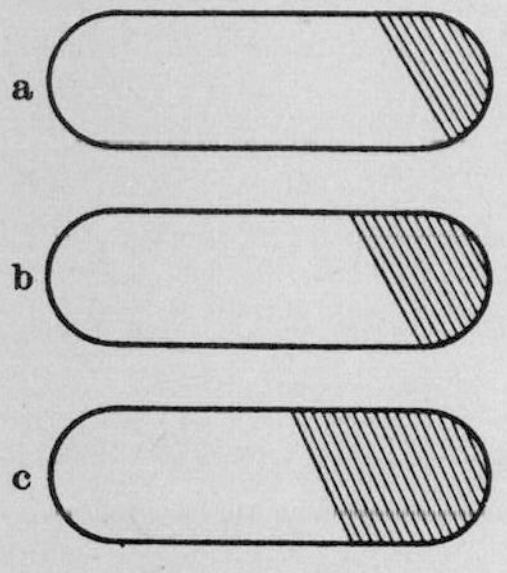

FIGURE 4

The actual figures used were drawn on medium gray cards, about 6 × 11″ in size. The contours were drawn with black India ink. The shaded areas were colored green, the remaining interior areas of the figures were colored white.

may also consist in *change* of some subregion of the object. In Figure 4 the variation is a change in color. St 4a contains a small green field; in the CFs the green is enlarged at the expense of the white field, the enlargement being greater in 4c than in 4b. CF 4b therefore contains a larger area which is identical with 4a than does 4c, and correspondingly it is more similar for 10 of 10 Os. Under Hypothesis I the *kind* of change is not specified. Only the amount of identical area or the number of identical parts in each CF need be considered to predict the outcome of the experiment, regardless of whether the change consists in an addition of parts, a subtraction of parts, or a qualitative change of parts. Of course, qualitative changes can often be thought of as combinations of addition and subtraction.

In experimental Figure 5a, b, c, the number of parts is the same in all three figures; the variation involves not the number of parts but rather their *position.* In 5b the slant of the right oblique line is changed; in 5c the slant of *both* obliques is

Measurements (angle with the horizontal):

	Left line	Right line
a	68°	68°
b	68°	56°
c	80°	56°

FIGURE 5

changed. Even though all three figures contain the same number of parts they differ in that in 5b a larger area, the middle and left lines, is completely congruent with the corresponding area of the St, whereas in 5c only the middle line remains identical. In accordance with the greater amount of identical area in 5b, the result is 5a $\sim$ b $\nsim$ c for 10 out of 10 Os.

This calculation of similarity from the number or extent of identical areas is applicable only if it is possible for the two CFs to differ in the extent of the area which is identical with the St. There are instances in which that is not true, however.

In the CFs of Figure 6, four of the eight dots of the St were

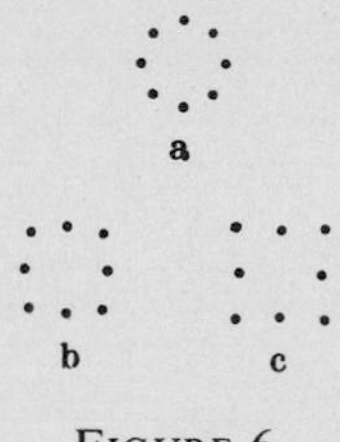

FIGURE 6

shifted outward: in CF 6c the same dots were shifted as in 6b, but over a larger distance. The two CFs have the same number of identical parts: in both cases four dots are identical and four are not. Nevertheless, 6b and 6c are not equally similar to 6a: rather, for 10 out of 10 Os, 6a $\sim$ b $\nsim$ c. It is, then, not enough to take the identical elements into consideration; it is also necessary to take into account the *extent of the change* in the nonidentical elements. The number of identical parts is the same, but among the nonidentical parts there is a difference in the degree of change from the original, and this difference seems to determine the degree of similarity.

The situation in Figure 7 is similar. The slant of the parallel lines is changed in both CFs, the change being greater in 7c than

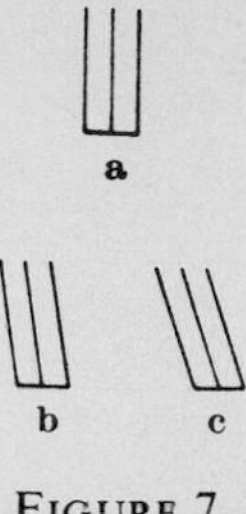

FIGURE 7

in 7b. The result is $7a \sim b \nsim c$ for 9 of 10 Os. Again there is no difference in the number of completely identical regions or parts: only the horizontal base line is identical in all three figures. The degree of similarity is determined by the degree to which the nonidentical parts differ from the St.

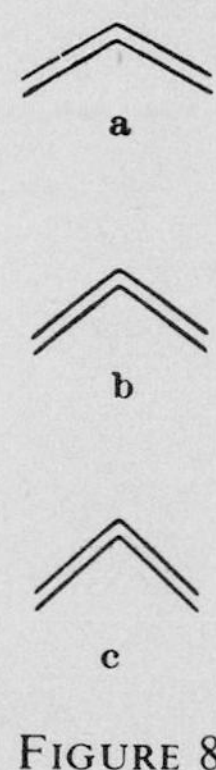

FIGURE 8

The same thing is true for Figure 8a, b, c, which is similarly constructed. In this case none of the parts of the CFs are in the same positions as they are in the St. Corresponding to the change in angle, $8a \sim b \nsim c$ for 14 of 15 Os.

These examples show that, in addition to the number of identical parts, it is also necessary to take into account the amount of the difference of the nonidentical parts from the St. This amplification of our previous formula is essential, because the difference of the nonidentical parts from the St, i.e., the difference in the distances in Experiment 6, and the difference in the directions in Experiments 7 and 8, cannot be reduced to equalities or inequalities of parts. Rather, it is a "similarity of the simple," in Stumpf's sense: similarities which are immediately given, not reducible to a calculation of the number of equal or identical parts.

5. HYPOTHESIS I: COUNTER EXAMPLES

The results of the experiments presented so far can be formulated as *Hypothesis I*:

The similarity between two figures varies directly with the number of parts which they have in common and inversely with the extent of change in the parts which are changed.

Obviously, in order to apply Hypothesis I it would have to be determined in what way the *number* of changed parts and the *degree of change* of parts should be reckoned against each other. Moreover, the hypothesis lacks rules for determining how different kinds of change should be taken into account: for instance, changes of angle against changes of color. However, if the principle of Hypothesis I is validated it should be easy to determine these rules empirically. The testing of Hypothesis I will therefore be restricted at first to cases in which it is possible to calculate similarity in spite of the lack of such empirical determinations. In the following experiments, all variants of previously used designs, the results contradict Hypothesis I.

When Figure 1a is compared with 1c and 1d, the result is $a \sim c \nsim d$ for 9 of 10 Os, even though in both CFs an equal number of parts has been subtracted, and, according to Hypothesis I, they should be equally similar to the St.

In Figure 2a, b, c, 2b contains more "new parts" than 2c. Nevertheless, the result is $2a \sim b \nsim c$ for 9 of 10 Os.

In Figure 9 the St is the same figure as 3a, and it is varied in the same way: by increasing the length of the short rays, in 9b

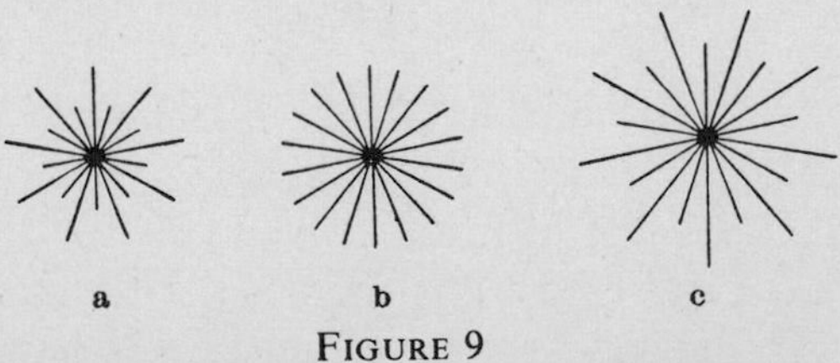

FIGURE 9

by a certain amount and in 9c by twice that amount. However, with the amount of increase chosen here the result is 9a $\sim$ c $\nsim$ b for 10 of 10 Os.

In Figure 27 (see below), the dot pattern is varied in the same way as in Figure 28: again in one CF some of the dots are enlarged and in the other all of the dots. In the case of Figure 27, however, 27c, the CF in which *all* the dots are enlarged, is more similar to the St for 9 of 11 Os.

In Figure 26 (see below), which is similar to Figure 4, some parts which were white in the St are colored green: in 26b part of the white area, in 26c the entire area. Even though the changed area in 26c is larger, this figure is more similar to the St for 11 of 12 Os.

In Figure 10, as in Figure 6, the change in 10b consists in a

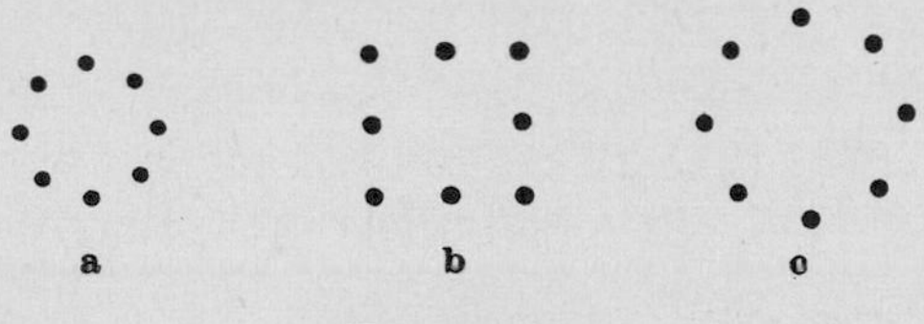

FIGURE 10

displacement of some of the dots outward. In 10c all the dots are shifted outward by the same amount. The number of changed parts is therefore twice as great in 10c as in 10b. In spite of this fact, 10a $\sim$ c $\nsim$ b for 10 of 10 Os.

In Figure 11 the horizontal line and the two oblique outer

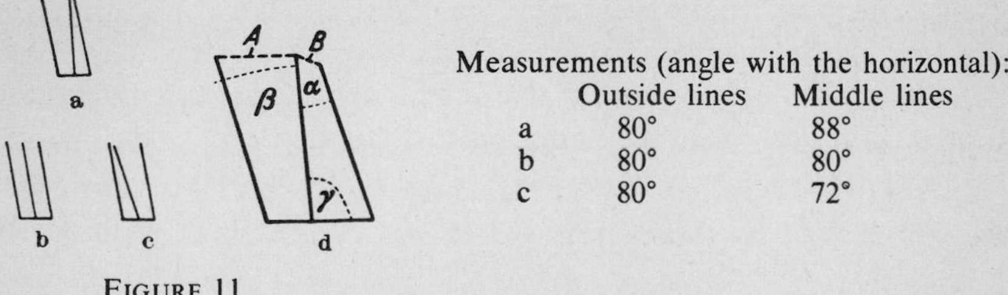

Measurements (angle with the horizontal):

	Outside lines	Middle lines
a	80°	88°
b	80°	80°
c	80°	72°

FIGURE 11

lines are the same in all three figures. The slant of the middle line here is the same as in the corresponding figures of Figure 7. Therefore, in both CFs the part represented by the middle line is different from the corresponding part of the St, and the variation is smaller in 11b than in 11c: nevertheless, 11c is more similar to the St for 8 of 10 Os, one O feels unable to make a judgment, and one considers 11b more similar than 11c.

6. INADEQUACY OF HYPOTHESIS I

Clearly, Hypothesis I is not adequate to account for these experimental results. Its range of applicability is restricted to certain special cases, which, however, cannot be identified at this point. If "identity of parts" has nevertheless been generally and widely assumed to be governing, it is surely because the deficiencies of this formulation do not become obvious until it is quantified, as it was in Hypothesis I. The destruction of the identity of subregions certainly tends to decrease similarity. But identical changes of parts can in one case lead to a profound change of the over-all figure while in another case they are hardly noticeable, and even quantitatively larger changes of parts do not always correspond to a larger loss of similarity for the whole. This fact has occasionally been noticed, but the suggestions for improving the hypothesis usually do not stand up under scrutiny. Thus Clauberg and Dubislav (1923) give, in addition to the already quoted definition, another one, representative of a number of similar, less concise formulations. "Objects which have enough qualities in common may be called similar." Now it is much more difficult to make an inventory of common qualities than of identical parts. The reason for this is the lack of definition of the concept of quality. One way to make this concept more definite is to consider as qualities only those geometric or qualitative parameters of single parts or subregions which define them as isolated entities "in themselves," as for instance the size of the dots in Figures 28 and 27, the length of the lines in Figures 2, 3, and 9, and the coloring of the subregions in Figures 4 and 26. These are uniquely defined, but obviously this solution leads only to a more precise version of Hypothesis I. In fact, this version coincides with the elaboration of this hypothesis formulated above in section 4 and shown to be inadequate by the experiments described in the present section.

In what follows the analysis turns to properties *which are not those of subregions or parts* (which do not characterize the subregion in itself as an isolated entity), that is, to the investigation of the role of whole qualities in determining similarity.

2

SIMILARITY AS IDENTITY OF RELATIONS: HYPOTHESIS II

7. THE SIGNIFICANCE OF RELATIONS

Various observations in perception, known to the older schools of psychology, directed attention to the role played by the *relations between parts.* Relations, as opposed to isolated parts and their properties as considered under Hypothesis I, are functions of the entire figure, or at least of large subregions. Of the relations, attention was focused particularly on the special case of objects having the *same proportions, i.e., the same ratio of measurements of the parts or of their distribution.* This proportionality implies identical angles. In fact, two configurations having the same proportions, especially if they are rich in detail, are in favorable cases not only similar but, in spite of change in size and quality, may even appear as identical when tested by recognition. We therefore focus particularly on this special type of relations, which corresponds to the mathematical concept of similarity. (See Mach, 1906, p. 108; Ebbinghaus, 1911, pp. 49f.; Stumpf, 1883; Ehrenfels, 1890; Cornelius, 1897; and many others.)

A theory in which similarity is explained by mathematical proportionality represents an extreme means of avoiding the piecemeal approach characteristic of Hypothesis I. Mach emphasized that *with even the slightest degree* of such change *no identical part is left*—as is required by Hypothesis I. Rather, the change is always a change of the entire figure.

8. HYPOTHESIS II

Of the experiments already reported several point to the effect of mathematical proportionality, especially those experiments which failed to support Hypothesis I: for instance, Experiment 2a, b, c, where only in the more similar CF, 2b, are the lengths of the rays in the same proportion as in the St; likewise Experiment 10, where in the more similar CF the proportion of the distances between the dots is preserved. The same thing can be said of Experiments 3 and 6, although they are also compatible with Hypothesis I. While in these two experiments the ratios of the lengths of the lines and the proportions of the distances between the dots in the more similar CF are not those of the St, they are more nearly so than in the less similar CF.

There are, then, cases in which greater similarity corresponds to better agreement in the proportions among those cases which can be explained according to Hypothesis I as well as among cases which cannot. If the correspondence demonstrated in these few instances is a general condition for similarity, the result is the following *Hypothesis II:*

Proportional changes of all parts of a figure result in a more similar figure than disproportional changes. In the case of disproportional changes, the smaller the deviation from proportionality, the greater the similarity.

9. GENERALIZATION OF HYPOTHESIS II

Hypothesis II requires some generalizations to account for certain *qualitative changes* such as changes of color. Here a suggestion presents itself that is in the spirit of Hypothesis II: to define a "proportionality" for changes in color which corresponds to that of form, rather after the manner in which a transposition is made from one key to another in music. Thus the results of Experiment 26 can be explained by Hypothesis II if it is agreed that changes of color, like changes of form, must be made in the entire region in the same way. It is not the single isolated element of color but the entire *color relationship* that must be preserved. According to this stipulation, CF 26c in Experiment 26 is mathematically favored because, just as in the St, all parts are "of equal color." Experiment 4 can likewise be brought under Hypothesis II: the color proportions are disturbed in both CFs, but in c obviously more than in b; therefore, b should be more similar to the St, as the experimental results showed.

The details of the indicated generalization are essentially matters for empirical determination. To the extent that fundamental difficulties arise, they seem to be of the same kind as those which will be treated below in connection with proportionality of form. I shall therefore confine the discussion of proportionality of qualities to these few examples and remarks.

Another supplementary rule is necessary if *all* the figures to be compared are proportional to one another, as for instance in Experiment 2a, b, d. Strictly speaking, it is not possible to explain this case by Hypothesis II alone; one must have recourse to Hypothesis I as well. But this difficulty can also be removed in a more natural way, already implied, by enlarging the range of application of Hypothesis II. It is merely necessary to require the preservation, if possible, of the proportions that obtain between the figure and its *surroundings,* such as the margin of the paper or even the observer himself. This generalization of the range of proportions will be enough to explain the results of experiments such as 2a, b, d.

10. PROBLEMS OF ASSIGNING HOMOLOGOUS PARTS IN EXPERIMENT 11

There are difficulties in the explanation of the results of Experiment 11 by Hypothesis II. The variation in this experiment consists only in the slant of the middle line. In CF 11b the middle line is inclined to the left by 8°; in 11c, the more similar CF, it is inclined to the left by an additional 8°. The lengths, and therefore the relationships between the lengths of the lines, are unchanged, while the angles are changed in the same direction. Obviously, then, the proportions of distances of homologous points are more disturbed in 11c. But a $\sim$ c $\nsim$ b. The hypothesis therefore fails.

The solution of this difficulty requires careful analysis of the meaning of Hypothesis II. It was conceived so as to take into account the fact that phenomenal similarity generally parallels geometric similarity. Mach seems to have been the first to pose the question as to the basis of this effect, which is by no means obvious.[1] He based his theory on observations about similarity when a figure is rotated. He assumed that the reason for similar-

[1] That a "simple relation of two objects for the intellect does not necessarily condition a similarity of sensation. may be perceived by comparing two triangles having respectively the sides a.b.c and a + m. b + m. c + m. The two triangles do not look alike" (Mach, 1906, p. 108).

ity is not the mathematical proportionality of all homologous distances nor the equality of the angles, but rather the agreement in *homologous directions,* and accordingly he thought that the "equal orientation" of the figures was prerequisite for recognizing the proportionality. Mach preferred to reduce the phenomenal similarity of geometrically similar figures to the *identity* of directions because with this "partial identity" of the figures–that is, in regard to directions–these phenomena could be reduced to Hypothesis I. However, this reduction is subject to the same objections which were developed against Hypothesis I in the preceding chapter. And, in fact, it does not lead to the correct result in our example, Experiment 11. Our reason for considering Hypothesis II was precisely the possibility of including the relations between the parts of the figures in the calculation. If we base our hypothesis not on the characteristics of individual parts but on their relationships, we have to start from the *proportions of distances* instead of from the distances and lengths of lines, and from the *relationship of directions* instead of from the directions. That means that we have to consider the *differences* of homologous directions, i.e., homologous angles.

To carry out this analysis on Figure 11, we will designate the angle between the right and the middle lines as α, the angle between the left and the middle line as β, and the angle between the right half of the horizontal line and the middle line as γ, as shown in the sketch 11d. The sizes of the angles in all three figures are shown in Table 1. In 11b, all three angles differ from those of the St. Figure 11c differs only in angle γ; the absolute values of α and β are the same as in the St. However, this latter statement is true only with a reservation: angle α in 11a has a sense opposite to that in 11c. In 11a the angle opens downward; in 11c it opens toward the top. And the corresponding is true for angle β. This is indicated in the table by the minus signs.

TABLE 1

	α	β	γ
11a	8	–8	92
11b	0	0	100
11c	–8	8	108

If one thinks this is merely a bit of mathematical trickery, he need only consider the ratios of lengths. If one considers, for instance, the distance between the endpoints of the slanted lines, labeled A and B in Figure 11d, in their relationship to other lines in the figure, the differences which had disappeared by considering the *absolute* sizes of angles are again apparent.

As far as the angles are concerned the *left* side of 11a and the *right* side of 11c correspond to one another; and in the ratios of homologous parts the left side of 11a and the right side of 11c likewise correspond–almost. This means that Hypothesis II applies, provided that one considers the left side of 11a homologous to the right side of 11c and the right side of 11a homologous to the left side of 11c. This situation is remarkable since to a naïve observer this view of the homology is the natural one, even though, as we have seen, mathematically it is not warranted. From the point of view of "function"[2] the left line of 11a is homologous to the right line of 11c as "a single line," and correspondingly the "pair" made up of the other two lines. On the basis of these assignments of homology, Hypothesis II furnishes the correct result; on the basis of the *mathematically* correct assignment, on the other hand, 11a and 11c differ more from each other than do 11a and 11b. Hypothesis II does not, however, contain or even imply any principle that would lead to the assignment of homology according to "function."

11. FURTHER PROBLEMS OF ASSIGNMENT OF HOMOLOGY

Difficulties in the assignment of homology of parts, although less obvious ones, also arise in figures of the type of Experiment 9.

In the similar CF, 9c, the ratio of the lengths of the long and short rays is approximately the same as that of the St, 9a; but the long rays are in fact parallel to the short rays of 9a, as can be seen from the description of the construction of the figure.[3] According to the point of view adopted in connection with Experiment 11, and also according to the geometrical concept of simi-

[2] For the significance of the function of parts see below, Chapter 4, as well as Wertheimer (1923) and Ternus (1926).

[3] See section 5. Note, for example, the two rays of 9a and 9c directed straight up.

larity, there is of course no reason to take into account differences of orientation in space. However, as Mach discovered, *in general* the spatial orientation of a figure is by no means irrelevant. This is true at least for adults. In figures of the type of Figure 9 too, the importance of spatial orientation becomes apparent if the number of rays is decreased so that the differences in the direction of homologous lines increase correspondingly.

As a rule, difficulties in the assignment of homology arise whenever parts are either *added to or taken away from* a given figure. Exceptions such as Experiment 9, or Experiment 2, are possible only if the addition or subtraction constitutes in effect a proportional or nearly proportional change. These exceptions, in addition to such proportionality, are always tied to an exchange in homology relations. In Experiment 9 that assignment in which the short rays of 9a are considered as homologous to the short rays of 9c is the most natural, even though "genetically" and according to orientation in space it is the long rays of 9a which correspond to the short rays of 9c. In this case, too, we are dealing with *functional homology.*

These experiments do not, however, represent the general case, such as, for instance, Experiment 1a, b, c. Here the differences in the number of parts affect even the possibility of assigning homology. No matter how the parts are assigned, for some parts of 1a there are no homologues in the comparison figures. The method of assigning homology used up to now cannot be applied here.

This problem might be solved by considering the *lack of relations* that occurs when parts are subtracted as a diminution of similarity. This expedient, however, amounts to a return to Hypothesis I, since the number of missing relations varies directly with the number of subtracted parts. And the arguments against Hypothesis I are also applicable to this new suggestion. It already meets with difficulties in Experiment 1a, c, d. The number of parts is the same in 1c and 1d, and thus the number of relations in the two figures is also the same. And the existing differences in the arrangements cannot be taken into account without postulating further rules.

Still more obvious is the failure of this assumption in Experiment 30. In both CFs 30b and c one half of the dots have been taken away. Consequently neither Hypothesis I nor Hypothesis II furnishes a criterion for decision, Hypothesis II not even if it is translated into Hypothesis I as applied to relations. Nevertheless, the outcome of the experiment is very clearly a ~ b ≁ c (10 out of 10 Os). Going by the number of the relations between the remaining dots in each figure, the result should have been equality, that is, equal degrees of loss of similarity to or change from 30a.

The same is true of Experiment 13a, b, c. Both CFs are derived from the zigzag arrangement of 13a by taking away two dots, and thus here again an equal number of relations is preserved in each CF. Nevertheless, the experiment shows very definitely that 13a ~ c ≁ b (7 out of 8 Os).

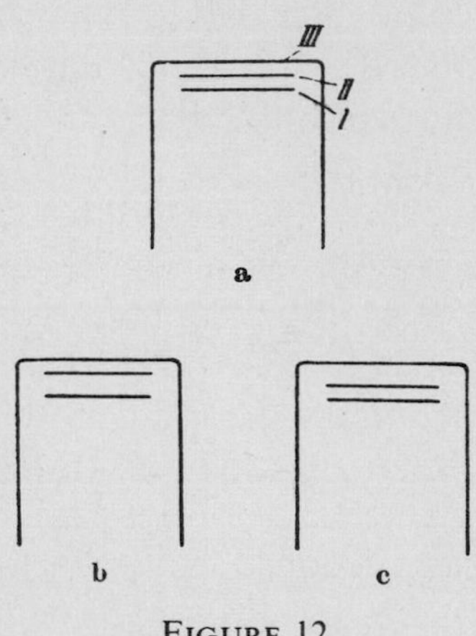

FIGURE 12

12. CASES IN WHICH HYPOTHESIS II FAILS

Hypothesis II is often in contradiction with experimental results even when there is no problem of assignment of homology. Figure 12 is such an instance. We designate the three parts of Figure 12 as I, II, and III, as shown in Figure 12a. In the St, 12a, the distance from I to II is as large as the distance from II to the horizontal part of III. In CF 12b the distance between I and II has been increased and the distance between II and III is unchanged from the St; in 12c the distance between II and III has been increased as much as that between I and II in CF 12b, while the distance between I and II is the same as in the St. In

12b the relations between I and II and between I and III are disturbed, while that between II and III is preserved; in 12c the relations between I and III and between II and III are disturbed while that between I and II is preserved. Obviously, according to the number of disturbed relationships between the three elements, the two CFs are equivalent. The experiment, however, results conclusively in 12a $\sim$ c $\not\sim$ b (9 of 10 Os). This experiment shows that it will not do to consider merely the *number* of disturbed relationships, and suggests the necessity of ascribing *different weights to different relations,* if indeed Hypothesis II can be salvaged at all. By making the assumption that preservation of the relationship between I and II is here *more important* than the preservation of the relationship between I and III and between II and III, the experimental result could be covered by Hypothesis II. This assumption is also supported by the immediate impression of Figure 12. Lines I and II seem to form a closer unit with each other than either of them does with III.

To be able to apply Hypothesis II to this case it would be necessary to find a criterion for determining the *weight* of the various relationships. A suggestion about how to do this is implicit in Hypothesis II. If a reduction of proportionality results in a reduction of similarity, then in addition to the *number* of disturbed proportions one might also consider the *degree* of the disturbance. This generalization is similar to the generalization of Hypothesis I made in section 4. Even if the same number of proportions is disturbed, they still might be disturbed to different degrees. In order to take the degree of disturbance into account the following reasoning might be applied: if one of two measurements is changed, the greater the change from the original measurement, the greater the change in *proportion.* Applied, for instance, to the ratio of distances this means that changes which involve points which originally are near together affect the proportions most. Conversely, proportions are preserved better if the same absolute change is made between points which were far apart to begin with. Hypothesis II might then be enlarged by saying that, in the case of the same amount of shifting, the closer the points were to each other to begin with, the greater is the effect of the shift on similarity.

It is difficult to decide whether, according to this new rule, the change in the relationship between I and II in Experiment 12 should be given greater weight than the change in the relationship between II and III. The relationship between I and III is changed by the same amount in both CFs and therefore it can be disregarded here. In the St the distance from II to the horizontal part of III is the same as the distance from II to I, and the amount of the shift leading to 12b is the same as that leading to 12c.

It might be argued that, according to our rule, the shift of II in relation to the *horizontal part* of III and the shift of I in relation to II should have the same weights. In this case the experimental results would decide *against* Hypothesis II. Even though this argument does not seem convincing, it shows at least that even the amended Hypothesis II cannot handle all cases of difference in the weight of relationships.

In order to subject the *amendment* of Hypothesis II to another test, let us consider Experiment 38 (see below), in which the calculation can be performed unequivocally.

The dots of 38a are shifted in CF 38b as a unit, by tilting both sides slightly from the vertical position; the distances between neighboring dots along the lines are same as in the St. Conversely, in CF 38c only the distances of the dots from their neighbors have been changed while the direction of the lines formed by the dots is vertical, as in the St. The absolute amount of shift in the two CFs is very nearly the same. If our enlargement of Hypothesis II were correct, the change in the distances between neighboring dots should have far more effect, and 38c should be less similar to the St. But the experiment has the opposite result for 18 of 20 Os.

13. RELATIONS OF HIGHER ORDER

It is an attractive conjecture that among the relationships of the parts which psychologically make up a whole the dominant role is played by relations of *higher order,* i.e., relations of relations; that these are the "most characteristic" relations. Undoubtedly there are cases in which this is true (see for instance the consideration of this possibility by Spearman [1925]). One might therefore consider putting the role of relations of higher order to the test. However, the deficiencies of the relational hypothesis, particularly the problems of homology, would arise again with higher-order relationships. Nor would the use of higher-order relations supply a means for taking into account differences in the weight of relations of the *same* order. It can be shown that the transition to relations of relations, and to even higher orders, does not lead to changes in the relational system which would in effect indicate the difference in the weight of relations. Important and unimportant relations are equally raised to higher orders. (I have made such a calculation, but presentation of it would take up too much space. See also section 24 and especially section 39, No. 2.) This is not to deny that among the relations of higher order which are not considered here there might be some whose preservation would enhance similarity. But this, too, applies not to all but only to some relations of some figures, just as is true of the first-order relations.

14. HYPOTHESIS II AS A VARIANT OF HYPOTHESIS I

Up to now this investigation has shown both Hypothesis I and Hypothesis II to be wanting. To some extent it appears that the deficiencies of both hypotheses can be traced to a common defect. Consider, for instance, Experiment 13; Hypothesis I would

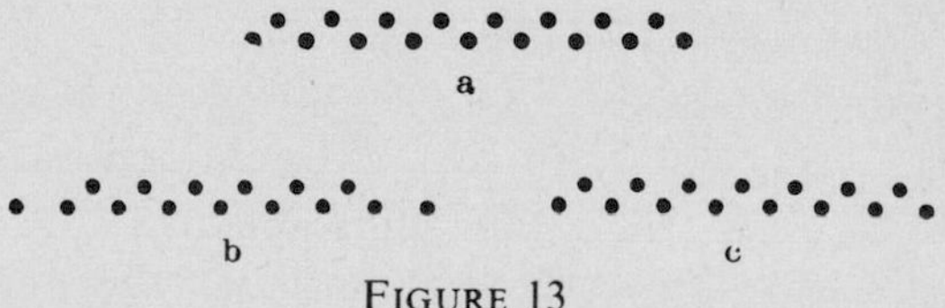

FIGURE 13

predict equal similarity, because in both CFs, 13b and c, two dots have been removed. But the experimental results contradict the hypothesis. And Hypothesis II fails in essentially the same way, as was shown in section 11. Now, if we look at these figures intuitively, the idea suggests itself that we consider as the "real" elementary parts not the dots themselves but rather their oblique connections. Translated into the language of Hypothesis II, this means that the relation between any two dots in an adjoining position is dominant over all relations between dots in other relative positions. As we have previously spoken of functional homology, so we might here introduce the notion of a functional weight of relations. According to this, in 13b four dominant relations have dropped out, whereas in 13c only two are missing. By adopting this correction, agreement of the hypothesis with the experimental results has once more been restored. But this is no improvement over Hypothesis I. If one treats the oblique connections between neighboring dots as parts, in the meaning of parts in Hypothesis I, then, according to Hypothesis I too, four parts have dropped out in 13b as against only two parts in 13c. Thus in such cases Hypothesis II is nothing more than a variant of Hypothesis I. Going over to the relations does not sharpen the distinction between relevant and irrelevant attributes. Of course, up to now Hypothesis II has been tested only by experiments in which either both CFs were proportional to the original, as in Experiment 2, or neither, as in Experiments 1, 11, 12, 13, and 38. However, it seems that the situation to which Hypothesis II is most appropriately applied is that in which a proportional CF competes with a disproportional CF. In such cases, there are neither problems of homology nor problems of the weight of relations, because in one of the CFs—the proportional one—all relations remain unchanged from the St. This is the case that will be examined in the following chapter.

3

SIMILARITY WITH ENLARGEMENT: MATERIAL AND FORM

15. THE BASIC EXPERIMENT

So far we have assumed that in Experiment 10 the CF 10c represents a proportional enlargement of the St. This is true, however, only if the dots which make up these figures are considered to be extensionless, like mathematical points. To construct a *mathematically* similar CF for the St, 10a, would require enlarging the dots in the proportion of $1/\sqrt{2}$, that is, 1/1.4, the amount by which the distances between the dots are enlarged. Figure 14 shows a strictly proportional enlargement of a figure

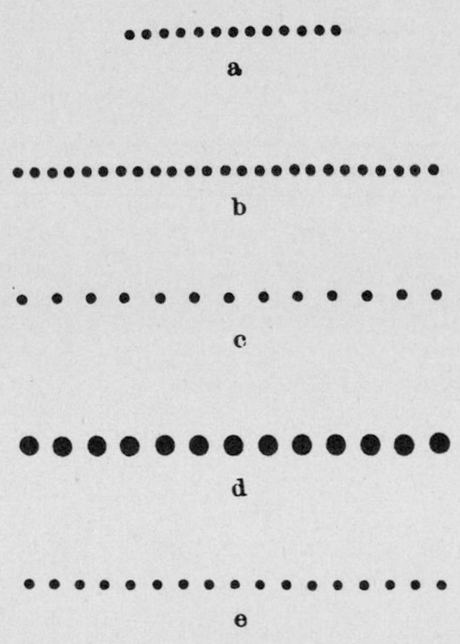

FIGURE 14

and also, for comparison, figures enlarged on the same scale in which the dots were not proportionally enlarged.

TABLE 2

Number of Os Choosing	1st comparison				2nd comparison			3rd comparison	
	b	e	d	c	b	d	c	d	c
in 1st place	**6**	2	2	0	**8**	2	0	5	5
in 2nd place	1	**6**	2	1	2	3	5	5	5
in 3rd place	2.5	1	**4**	2.5	0	**5**	**5**		
in 4th place	0.5	1	2	**6.5**					

The St is a row of dots. All the CFs are twice as long, but only in 14d have all measurements been doubled, including the size of the dots. In 14c the distance between the dots has been doubled; the diameter of the dots is the same as in the St. In 14b and e likewise the dots have not been enlarged. In 14b the distance between dots is the same as in the St. In 14e the distance between dots is larger than in 14b but smaller than in 14c: the distance was so chosen that the gaps between two dots are the same size as in 14d. The Os were asked, "Which CF is the most similar?" After the O had made a decision the chosen CF was removed and the same question was asked about the remaining CFs. Table 2 shows in the column "1st comparison" how often each CF was chosen first, second, third, or fourth. When two CFs appeared equally similar, each was given half credit for that place and the following one. The maxima of the choices of each CF are printed in the table in boldface. For instance, CF 14e was placed most frequently in second place (6 of 10 Os).

The large number of CFs presented in this experiment seemed to be confusing. Judging by the Os' behavior, the ranking of 14d and 14e was particularly questionable. CF 14d, moreover, is the figure which has the lowest maximum. Therefore, in a second comparison, CF 14e was omitted. The results are shown in Table 2 in the column "2nd comparison." In a third comparison, shown in the last column of Table 2, only 14c and d were compared. Ten Os participated in each comparison.

In regard to the proportionally enlarged CF the experimental results by no means support Hypothesis II. In the first comparison, 14d is ranked next to last; in the other two comparisons 14d and c are given approximately equal rank, and are judged by the majority of Os to be less similar than 14b. The essential result of the experiment is the superiority of 14b and, to a lesser extent, 14e. In neither of these CFs is the diameter of the dots or the distance between them proportional to the St. They also differ from the St in the number of dots, so that it is not even possible to determine homology uniquely. Nevertheless, as the table shows, they are more similar to the St than the proportional CF, 14d. The preference for 14b and e over 14d greatly surpasses the slight superiority of 14d over c in the three comparisons. This suggests that a very strong effect must be at work here, which, in fact, could be demonstrated in a number of additional patterns.

16. FURTHER EXPERIMENTS

In Experiment 15a, b, c, CF 15c is a proportional enlargement

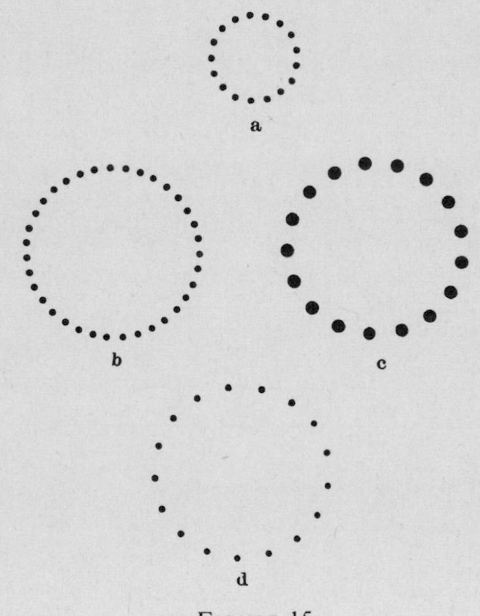

FIGURE 15

of 15a; in 15b the dots were not enlarged proportionally and their number was increased. Here too the proportionally enlarged CF is the less similar for 10 out of 10 Os.

In Experiment 16 the St is an ordinary line; in one CF, 16b, it has been doubled in both length and width, whereas in the other CF, 16c, only the length has been doubled. The result was

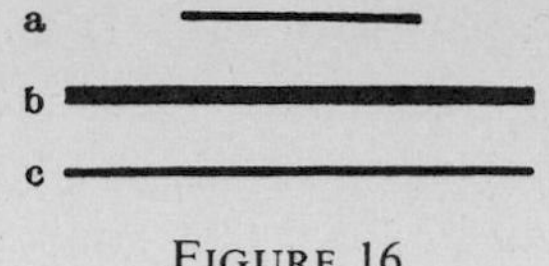

FIGURE 16

16a ∼ c ≁ b for 10 of 10 Os. The triple enlargement shown in Experiment 17 resulted in a ∼ c ≁ b for 9 of 10 Os.

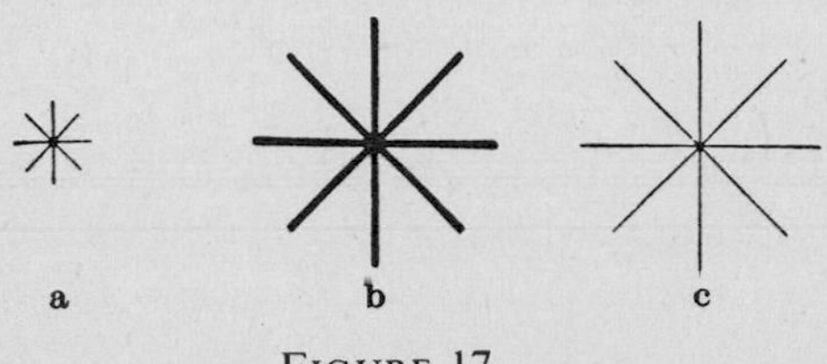

FIGURE 17

Taking Hypothesis II literally, there is no doubt that it fails in these cases. However, one might consider the possibility that these are borderline situations, special conditions for which the rule has to be modified. Rubin (1921) has found that thin lines and small dots may appear to be without extension. This observation might lead to an explanation of our experimental results by the assumption that phenomenally our dots and lines have no width or extension, if it were further assumed that phenomenally nonexistent attributes are exempt from the requirement of Hypothesis II for proportional enlargement. This would mean that proportionality would be required only for the remaining geometrical parameters.

But in the form stated this is not an acceptable explanation of our findings. The dots here are large and obvious and phenomenally surely not without extension.[1] The Os were by no means unaware of the difference in the sizes of the dots. The same is true for the line in Experiment 16. Its thickness may be considerable. In one experiment (figures not shown) the St was a rectangle 5 mm. high and 10 cm. long. Even then, with an enlargement of 1:2, the CF of the same width as the St appeared more similar

[1] The diameter of the black dots used in these experiments was 5.5 mm.; the thickness of the line was 1 mm. The spaces between the dots were 4 mm. in one instance, more in all the others. Viewing distance was 30 to 80 cm.; in experiments with successive presentation it was 2 m. See also section 20.

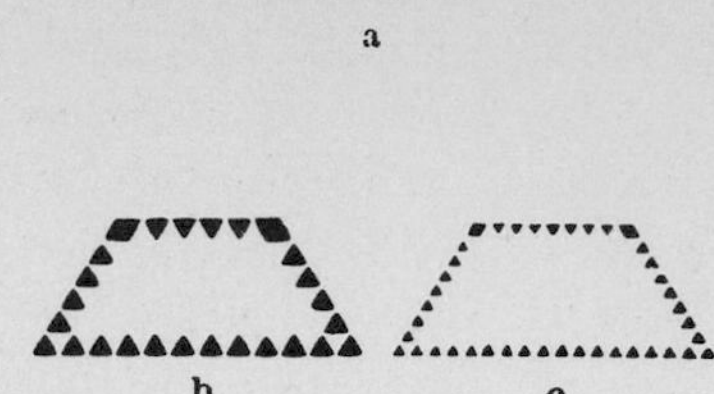

FIGURE 18

for 10 of 10 Os, in spite of the marked discrepancy in the proportions of the sides.

The same result was found in Experiment 18, where the elements–small triangles–certainly cannot be considered as quasi-extensionless points. Here too the proportionally enlarged CF, 18b, was less similar for 8 of 10 Os.

Finally, even if we grant for the moment that the lines and dots have no extension, it is still not explained that similarity, furthermore, does not depend on the *distances* between the dots–in Experiment 14–which in the more similar CF were likewise not proportional to the St. These distances surely are not without extension; furthermore, variations of the distance in Experiment 14 undoubtedly caused differences in similarity.

17. MATERIAL AND FORM: RULE 1

It is possible to interpret the experimental results by noting that there is, in the Sts of Experiments 14, 15, and 18, a sharp phenomenal separation between the *over-all form* and the *material* from which the form is constructed. [2] The phenomenal forms in these experiments are line, circle, and trapezoid. The material consists of dots at certain distances and chains of triangles. Mathematically it is of course possible to establish ratios between size of dots and length of line, side of the triangles and side of the trapezoid, and in general between some measurement characteristic of the material and some measurement characteristic of the form, and the ratios are just as much ratios as those between the four sides of the trapezoids. But psychologically these ratios

[2] [This is the same distinction as that between form and mode made by Asch, Ceraso, and Heimer (1960).–E.G.]

are no more realized than, say, the ratio between the thickness of a line and the width of the sheet of paper on which the line happens to be drawn. These ratios do not have even indirect significance for the form, as do, for instance, those proportions which constitute the curvature of the dotted circle, or the rectilinearity of the line in Experiment 14. These proportions exist merely as a *geometrical possibility, not as a phenomenal reality.* Correspondingly, similarity is not affected in any way whatsoever if they are disturbed. On the other hand, similarity is decreased if *"real" measurements of the material are changed.*

It seems that Mach must have at least sensed this distinction, because in his demonstrations of optical similarity he used only solid black figures whose borders are formed by the discontinuity of brightness between the black figure and the white paper, which phenomenally is without extension.

As the basis for this phenomenal description the following rule suggests itself for figures in which there is a phenomenal separation into material and form.

Rule 1: The form is best preserved by proportional enlargement; material properties are best preserved by keeping the measurements of the material elements constant.

The second half of this rule corresponds only superficially or apparently to Hypothesis I. In CFs such as the circles of Experiment 15, it is not particular, individual elements of the St which recur. Furthermore, a particular measurement in 15b does not correspond to any particular measurement in 15a, as can be seen if one tries to match up individual elements or distances in the two figures. The identity lies in the *type of arrangement.* This was expressed in many spontaneous remarks of the Os. A CF with changed distances between the dots appeared as "too dense," "too loose," "too wide." One O stated as his criterion that "it has to have a similar compactness, density." "Dense" and "loose" in these figures are *properties of the material.* "The form is always the same."

18. TESTING RULE 1

In the case of dot figures such as Figures 14 and 15, the size of and distance between the dots are characteristics of the material. The question whether constancy in the characteristics of the material results in maximum similarity was then tested in detail for the *distance between the dots* in Experiment 19. The St was a circle with a diameter of 8 cm. and consisting of 17 dots. The six

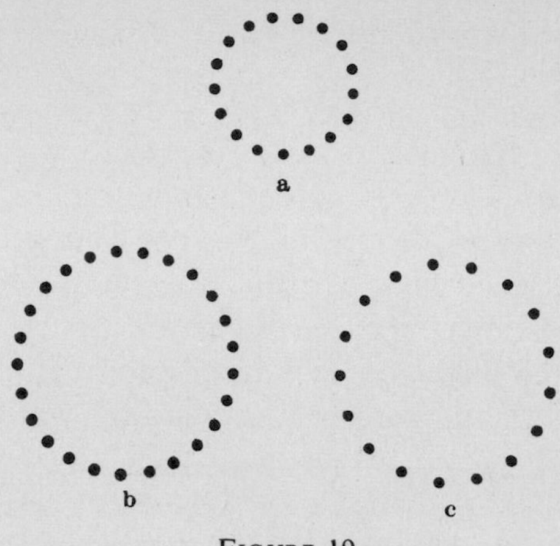

FIGURE 19

CFs each had a diameter of 12 cm. and were made up of dots of the same size as those in the St. The numbers of dots in the comparison circles were 15, 17 (= Figure 19c), 19, 22, 25 (= Figure 19b), and 29. In this experiment the CFs will be designated as "CF 22," etc., according to the number of dots. In CF 25 the absolute distance between dots was nearly the same as in the St on the scale of enlargment of 2:3 used. Of 10 Os, 4 chose CF 25, 2 each CF 22 and 29, 1 O could not decide between CFs 22 and 19, and 1 chose CF 15 as most similar to the St. No O chose CF 17, which had the same number of dots as the St and which, apart from the diameter of the dots, was proportional to the St. The maximum of choices lay with CF 25; the average number of dots in the CFs chosen, i.e, the arithmetic mean, was 23.75. This number was calculated to obtain a convenient numerical expression of the results. This outcome, then, conforms to Rule 1, since the circle in which the distance between dots is most nearly the same as in the St is chosen most frequently, both on the average and in absolute numbers. The agreement is still better if the rank order of choices is taken into account. For instance, the O whose first choice was CF 15, which deviates most from the average, put CF 25 in second place.

A similar result was obtained with the same St (= Figure 15a, which was in actuality identical with 19a) and comparison figures twice as large as the St. In this case Rule 1 would predict the maximum similarity for CF 35 (= Figure 15b). However, CF 29, which is one step lower, was chosen by 8 of 17 Os. Three Os did choose CF 35, and 3 chose the next step higher, CF 42; 2 chose CF 25, and 1 chose CF 13. No O chose 17 (= Figure 15d) or 21. The maximum of choices is one step lower than was expected according to Rule 1; the *average* number of dots chosen is 31.53, about midway between CF 29 and a CF 34 (not offered) which should have been the most similar to the St by Rule 1.

If the measurements that pertain to the material are not phenomenally related to the measurements that pertain to the form, then the requirement that they be kept *constant* if the form is changed is the simplest rule conceivable. That is not meant to exclude modifications of this rule if the scale of enlargement is extreme or if the surrounding conditions deviate markedly from those used here.

19. CRITERIA FOR THE DIFFERENTIATION OF MATERIAL AND FORM: RULE 2

Rule 1 (Section 17) establishes a law of variation for a particular mode of change, namely enlargement, and particular conditions, namely phenomenal separation between material and form. However, in order to apply this rule it is necessary to find geometrical criteria for this phenomenal separation.[3]

The examples given so far suggest that a separation into material and form occurs not only in figures which consist of discrete elements. There may also be, as in Experiment 16, a separation between some measurements of a continuous structure. There the *thickness* of the line becomes a material property, while its length is perceived as a constituent of the form.

The one thing that the distances which go to make up the impression of material have in common is that they are all rela-

[3] [This is the type of quantitative study which Gestalt theorists have often been accused of neglecting, especially during the 1950s, when there were hopes that information theory might provide means of quantifying the too "subjective and qualitative formulation" of Gestalt principles (Hochberg and McAlister, 1953). Rule 2 is offered as an example of what can be and has been done by Gestalt theory.—E.G.]

tively small compared with the over-all dimensions of the figure. This is true of the size of the dots and the distances between them, the size of the small triangles, and the thickness of the lines. Furthermore, when the figure is composed of individual elements *their number is rather large.* This condition can be formulated as follows.

Rule 2: The phenomenal separation of material and form arises in the following manner: Characteristics of the design which (a) because of relative smallness are not phenomenally related to the over-all measurements of the figure as a whole, and which (b), in the case of discontinuity, are not individualized because of their large number, are relegated to the role of material.

20. TESTING RULE 2, ESPECIALLY 2a

The separation into material properties and form properties should disappear if one or both of the conditions specified in Rule 2 are not met. At the same time it would then be expected that, in general, the proportionally enlarged CF will be more similar to the St.

If the lines in Figure 16 are *shortened* so much that length and width fall within the same order of magnitude, the separation of length as a form property from width as a material property vanishes. The figures then no longer appear as lines but rather as rectangles or squares (Figure 20), as would be expected accord-

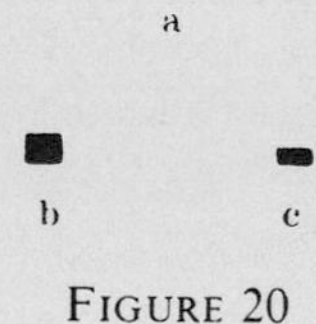

FIGURE 20

ing to Rule 2. Accordingly, for 7 of 8 Os, 20a $\sim$ b $\not\sim$ c, even though c is the same height as the St.

Figures 21 and 22 are parallel to Figures 18 and 14 respectively. The relative size and number of elements were so changed that neither condition postulated for a separation of material from form is met. Correspondingly, Experiment 21 results in a $\sim$ b $\not\sim$ c for 8 of 9 Os.

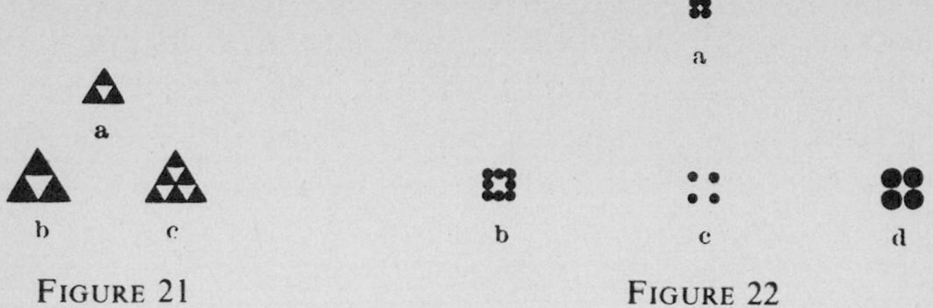

FIGURE 21 FIGURE 22

CFs 22b, c, and d are derived from 22a in the same way that CFs 14b, c, and d are derived from 14a. In this experiment, however, 22d is definitely the most similar. Of 10 Os, 5 decided for the rank order d, b, c, 3 for d, c, b, and 2 considered d as most similar and c and b as of equal rank.

By moving the dots of 22a farther apart (Figure 23a) we now

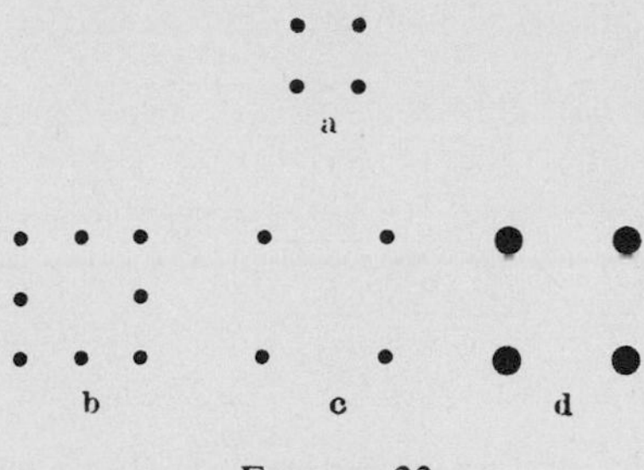

FIGURE 23

obtain a figure in which the extension of the *elements* is smaller in relation to the over-all figure than in Figure 22, while the extension of the *distance* between the dots is larger. Correspondingly, the size of the dots descends to the level of a material property while the distance between the dots enters into the experience of form. The preference in Experiment 22 for d should therefore decrease for the corresponding variation in Experiment 23, and instead of the equal ranking of 22b and c there should be, in Experiment 23, a preference for c over b. Of 10 Os, 5 decided for d, c, b, and 5 for c, d, b. Figure 23b has thus become decidedly the least similar, and 23c and d are of equal rank.

A comparison of the results of the last two experiments shows that for groupings which are composed of discrete elements it is possible to separate the effect of relative smallness–Rule 2a–from the other condition, the large number–Rule 2b. Relative smallness is to be considered an *independent* factor even if the figure is composed of many discrete elements. Experiments 22 and 23 confirm the validity of Rule 2a for the distance between and the size of the dots.

21. TESTING RULE 2b

The second factor which produces a separation into material and form, with its consequences for similarity in the case of enlargement, is, according to Rule 2, the *number* of elements which make up the figure. In figures which are composed of discrete elements, an increase in their number leads to a change in the function of the individual elements. If the number is small they are individual parts of the figure; as the number increases they lose individuality and become mere components of the material of the larger unit. On the other hand, the accumulation of elements creates a special impression of material which leads to more general structural properties: the "grain," the type of over-all arrangement, the density of the elements and irregularities in density. This can be visualized with rows of dots like those in Figure 14, by varying the dots so as to create places of accumulation. If a figure composed of many elements is enlarged it is to be expected that the *number* of elements will have to be increased, though the geometrical proportions of the elements relative to the whole of the design are lost in this process, if the structure of the over-all figure is to be preserved.

These considerations suggested tests using a figure which allows varying the number of elements without at the same time requiring a change in its over-all measurements.

The St, Figure 24a, is a rectangle made up of parallel lines. In both CFs the rectangle is enlarged in both width and height to twice the size of the St. In 24c the distance between the lines is the same as it is in the St, whereas in 24b this distance too is doubled. In 24c, then, the lines were increased in number as well as in length, whereas in 24b they were increased only in length. The result was 24a $\sim$ c $\nsim$ b for 9 of 12 Os.

In the next experiment, Figure 25, a rectangle of the same size is used, but in this case the St consists of only three parallel lines, as against seven in Figure 24. The CFs are derived according to the same principle as in Experiment 24. Now, however, it is

FIGURE 24 FIGURE 25

the CF with the same number of lines and the proportionally enlarged distances between them that is the more similar: 25a ∼ b ≁ c for 7.5 of 10 Os. *As is expected from Rule 2b, if the number of elements is small the enlargement of the figure must be proportional (25b), while if the elements are numerous an impression of material is created which is better rendered in an unproportionally enlarged CF (24c) than in a proportionally enlarged one.*

22. THE NUMBER OF ELEMENTS

It is not possible to designate a definite least number of elements necessary for the impression of material. Using similarity experiments as the criterion for the appearance of the impression of material, i.e., assuming that there is an impression of material if the unproportional CF is chosen, the situation is as follows: with few—up to about 6—elements, the proportional variant is likely to be chosen; therefore the impression of material is absent. With many elements—starting from about 9 to 11—it appears with great reliability. In between there is a region of gradual transition in which the results fluctuate. Here individual differences of Os, sets, attitudes, and small differences of observation have disproportionately large effects, in a way which can be determined in each instance only by special experimental methods devised for the purpose.

In addition to the subjective factors just mentioned, the structure of the figure also has considerable influence on the numerical dividing line. As a rule of thumb it may be said that the minimum number of elements required to produce the impression of material increases if the elements are arranged in subgroups.

Apparently the impression of material is related to the phenomenon which is customarily called attention span. The details described here are exactly paralleled in the investigations of this topic.[4]

It must be admitted that the effect of number cannot be *completely* isolated from the effect of linear extent (Rule 2a) because, for geometrical reasons, if the number of elements in any figure is increased the individual element must decrease in relative size; or else, as in Figure 24, the distance between the elements must decrease. If both these results are avoided, the over-all size of the figure will increase. In any case, the result is a decrease in the dimensions of the elements relative to those of the over-all figure.

Thus it is conceivable that the *relative diminution in the dimensions of elements,* described in Rule 2a, which inevitably accompanies an increase in the number of elements, by itself causes the separation into material and form which is certainly demonstrated in our experiments. Rule 2b, according to which the number of elements is an independent factor in this separation, is therefore not completely established. However, it certainly corresponds to the immediate subjective impression. To deny the role of number would require the reinterpretation of the observations on attention span and phenomenal number (Biemüller, 1930; Miller, 1956) in a corresponding manner.

23. REVIEW OF PREVIOUS EXPERIMENTS

The separation into material and form—as described by Rule 2—occurs whether a figure is varied by enlargement or in some other way. If this separation is taken into account the previous considerations require the following correction: Each geometric change should be examined with a view to determining whether it affects the impression of material, or of form, or the interplay of these two aspects of the design. Conceivably, Hypotheses I and II might not fail if they were applied only to the form of the designs.

[4] See especially Biemüller's observations (1930), which largely agree with the observations made here. [They anticipate what G. A. Miller (1956) has epitomized as "the magical number seven plus or minus two."—E.G.]

Even though this will not be found to be so, the possible corrections will be illustrated on a few cases to show how they are applied, which difficulties they solve, and which remain.

Thus we now have, in Figure 1, as forms, the triangles 1a, b, c, and, in d, a sort of rectangle topped by a small triangle. The material of the figures is a "filling with dots" or, more precisely, parallel rows of dots. The dots are the material of the rows, the rows the material for the whole figures. This means that here the material-form relationship exists in a hierarchy of two levels. The material component is unchanged; the variation involves only the form. For Hypothesis I the correction might mean that the hypothesis would not have to be applied to the number of individual dots but could apply instead to the total length of the horizontal rows or possibly to the total area of the figure. In that case, in Experiment 1a, c, d there is a slightly greater length of row and size of area in 1c, from which formally the "correct" result 1a $\sim$ c $\nsim$ d is obtained. The excess amounts to only about 10%, however, and this could hardly lead to the almost unanimous decision (9 out of 10 Os). In any case, there are enough instances in which the correction does not prevent the failure of Hypothesis I, e.g., Experiment 2a, b, c, and many others.

For Hypothesis II, the consideration of the separation into material and form is somewhat more successful. In Experiment 1a, b, c *the problem of homology is solved* since with respect to *form* the three figures are proportional; and, in Experiment 1a, c, d, the result a $\sim$ c $\nsim$ d is adequately explained by noting that, in form, a and c are proportional, whereas a and d are disproportional. The problem of homology in Experiment 9, briefly described earlier, is solved in a way which quite interestingly illuminates the mechanism of the correction. Figure 9a represents two circular stars made of rays, one inside the other, which are characterized by—in addition to their circularity—a certain ratio between the lengths of their radii. Each star is, as far as the material is concerned, made out of individual radii which are, somewhat like the dots in a dotted line, defined phenomenally by such things as their equality and their angular density, but not by their *individual* orientation in space. In this sense 9c is nearly proportional to 9a, with the same attributes as far as material is concerned.[5] To calculate this it is only necessary to consider the ratio between the rays in each figure. The directions of individual rays—like the locations of individual dots within a dotted line—are parameters neither of the material nor of the form. In respect to direction, all that matters is that the rays differ in direction by certain equal amounts.

The general validity of Hypothesis I is not affected by the enlargement of its range of application which was achieved by the correction, for instance, in Experiment 1 (p. 51). For Hypothesis II the correction solves problems of homology which arose in connection with material elements. This makes it possible to explain cases in which both CFs (for instance, Experiment 1a, b, c)—or at least one of them—are proportional to the St in form, even though the material elements cannot be related to each other as homologues. On the other hand, cases in which both CFs are disproportional are still not covered by Hypothesis II, either because the correction does not apply, as in Experiments 11 and 12, or because it has no effect, as in Experiment 38.

In Experiment 38 the correction results only in the recognition that CF 38c represents a change of material. This does not allow a conclusion regarding similarity. A change of form is by no means always more profound than a change of material. This topic will be covered more fully in Chapter 5.

[5] The description of material and form properties given here is not complete and is intended to give only essential details. It would have to be modified somewhat for 9c. Further investigation has shown that in order to obtain the same phenomenal "density" of rays in enlargements of figures of this type it is necessary to *increase* the number of rays. Furthermore, in form, 9c is not exactly proportional to 9a: the long rays are somewhat too short. Strictly speaking, 9c preserves neither the material nor the form of 9a with complete fidelity. But, compared with the much more drastic difference in the form of 9b, its imperfections do not matter much.

4

SIMILARITY AS CONSERVATION OF THE PHENOMENAL APPEARANCE: VARIATION OF STRUCTURE

24. THE RELEVANCE OF PHENOMENALLY REALIZED QUALITIES

The investigation of figures in which changes were not proportional amply demonstrated that not all relations between parts are of equal weight. However, we lack a general principle according to which different ranks might be assigned to different relations. For a few cases we found such a principle, which might be formulated thus: in tallying agreement in proportions, the ratios between parameters of material and of form should be disregarded. This principle was adequate for some cases, for instance when the change from St to CF was restricted to the relations which were to be excluded, as in Experiment 1a, b, c. However, as soon as the form is varied in *both* CFs the problem of different weight arises again and cannot be solved by either Hypothesis I or II.

Furthermore, it has become clear that in these cases it often makes no difference whether they are treated by Hypothesis I or Hypothesis II, whether the analysis is based on changed parts, changed distances, or changed relationships of distances (see, e.g., Experiments 11, 12, 13, 38). This, too, suggests that the defect of the hypotheses so far considered lies not in the kinds of characteristics considered but rather in the lack of a selective principle (see Matthaei, 1929, especially p. 7).

Finally, and this is decisive, in the individual case such criteria for selection appear intuitively, without effort, simply by looking at the figure. The only selective principle investigated in detail so far, the principle of separation of material and form, was arrived at intuitively.

These considerations suggest starting from the intuitive attributes of the structures to be compared and looking for the measure of difference in similarity in the change of *intuitive qualities,* in the change of what I will call *phenomenal appearance, picture, structure, or figure.*

Not that the "phenomenal picture" should be considered here as the ultimate entity, not open to further analysis, a position which has frequently and erroneously been ascribed to Gestalt theory (among many others, by Spearman, 1925, p. 216). Analysis of the phenomenal picture does not result in sets of relations of any particular order, but leads to properties of an entirely different kind. The connection between these properties and the just mentioned sets of relations is amenable to analysis. In fact, this connection has been investigated to some extent. But these properties are not identical with any set or subset of relations, as contemplated by Spearman (1925) and other associationists. The preceding chapter may serve as a paradigm for the analysis of the phenomenal picture as well as for the search for the connection between phenomenal attributes and geometrical parameters. Analysis of the phenomenal appearance revealed the existence of two groups of phenomenal qualities, those characterizing the material and those of form. Their significance for the impression of similarity is the subject of Rule 1. In addition, it was possible to determine which relations enter into the impression of material and which are responsible for the impression of form. This is expressed in Rule 2. Rule 1 could be correct even if the relationships embodied in Rule 2 should prove to be not quite correct as stated, or even if they were entirely unknown. Only Rule 1 makes a direct statement about similarity. Thus if we are looking for the source of similarity in the agreement of phenomenal qualities, our goal is to find rules like Rule 1. The knowledge of *which* ratios or other geometrical parameters are phenomenally effective, lead to phenomenal qualities, or are phenomenally realized, as I prefer to put it, that Rule 2 now makes available for certain cases, is only a means—useful though it may be—to this end.

The question to be posed, then, is: *Can the similarity of figures be reduced to differences and agreements of phenomenally realized qualities, as opposed to the logically constructible attributes?*

A. Variation of Grouping

25. Grouping according to the factor of similarity

The phenomenal appearance of a figure is roughly determined by its division into natural parts, by its *articulation.* Articulation in this narrow sense means only the way in which the figure is phenomenally divided into parts or, looked at from the point of view of the elements, the way in which the elements of the figure are *grouped.* We are well informed about the figural factors that determine grouping (Wertheimer, 1923). Armed with this knowledge we will investigate first the role of grouping in similarity. It is possible to vary a figure by geometrically *equal amounts* in such a way that the phenomenal grouping of the parts is either preserved or changed. Which of the two versions is more similar in comparable circumstances?

This question is examined in Experiments 26 and 27. In Experiment 26 the areas of the same color are grouped together into subunits according to Wertheimer's factor of similarity. In the more similar CF, 26c, this leads to one uniform area as in the

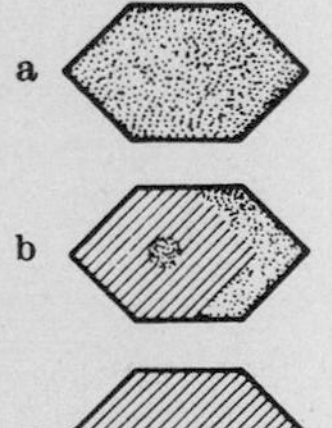

The actual figures used were drawn on medium gray cards about 6 × 9″ in size. The hexagonal contour was drawn with black India ink; the dotted areas were colored white, the shaded areas green.

Figure 26

St, whereas in 26b it creates two separate regions. Similarity corresponds to the agreement in grouping (homogeneity). Analogously, the dots in Experiment 27 are grouped in the same way in the St and CF 27c, as a hexagon, according to the "factor of good Gestalt." Those details of the grouping which are the same in all three figures need not concern us here. In CF 27b, howev-

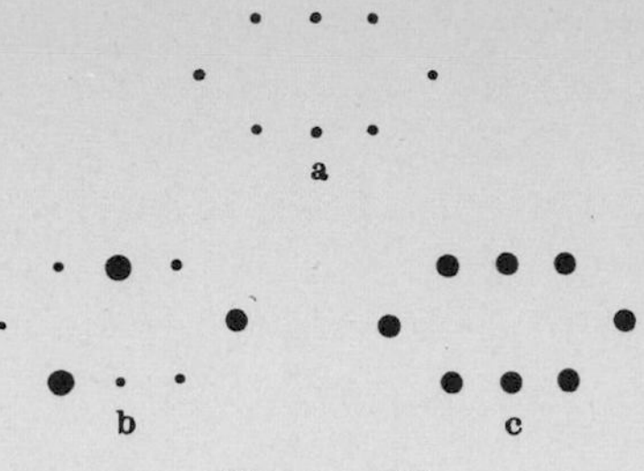

FIGURE 27

er, another, additional, grouping occurs, which competes with the original grouping according to the factor of similarity. In this figure three dots of a different size form a separate group which is not spontaneously visualized as a phenomenal grouping in the St.

In 27a and c, then, the grouping of the elements is the same, whereas in a and b it is not. Similarity corresponds to the difference in grouping, in the ordering of the elements into subgroups.

In order to derive the results of these two experiments from general rules, a law is needed according to which the absolute change of color in 26c and the uniform change of the size of the dots in 27c–both of which, after all, also represent phenomenal changes–can be considered as less extensive than changes in the organization of the elements into subunits. Such a law will be derived in Chapter 5, section 35. In both experiments it might appear that the derivation indicated here is merely an involved version of the explanation which could be given much more simply according to Hypothesis II (see section 9). In the less similar variant 26b the color proportions of the subregions are disturbed; in 27b the proportional relations among the dots. In the more similar variants both these proportions are preserved. There is a clear-cut difference between these two explanations, which is open to experimental decision. In Figures 26 and 27 the parts are grouped according to the factor of similarity. If the explanation proposed here is correct, only *equality* needs to be preserved because of its articulating function; proportions other than *equality* have no effect on grouping and therefore need not be preserved. The decision is possible by means of Experiment

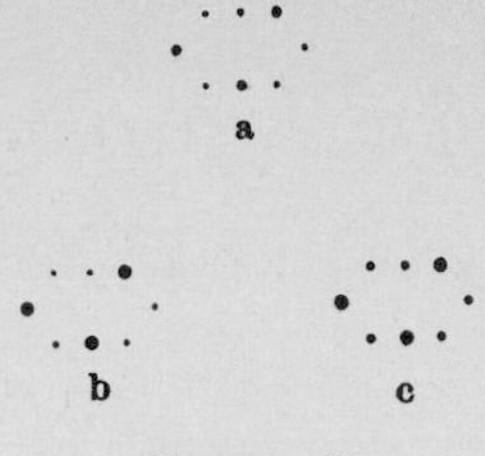

FIGURE 28

28. In this experiment the St already consists of dots of *unequal* size. In 28b only the larger dots are enlarged, and therefore the proportional relations among the dots are disturbed just as in 27b. In 28c both groups of dots are enlarged so that the proportional relations among them are the same as those of the St. Thus the proportions are preserved in 28c as they are in 27c; the grouping according to the factor of *similarity*, however, is now very nearly the same in all three figures of 28. In this respect 28b does not differ from the St, with which, in addition, it also shares five unchanged dots. According to Hypothesis II one should expect here, just as in Experiment 27, $a \sim c \nsim b$. The result, however, is $a \sim b \nsim c$ for 7 of 8 Os. When proportions deviate enough from 1/1, i.e., when the change does not represent a transition from equality to inequality and therefore to a different subdivision into parts, the conservation of proportional relations is less important than the conservation of absolute dot size (27b).

26. GROUPING ACCORDING TO OTHER FACTORS: RESULT

Consideration of the grouping of parts also supplies the explanation for Experiment 12 (p. 33). In 12a the factor of similarity forms a subunit of lines I and II which does not include III. The subdivision of 12a may be symbolized by the formula I II; III. The factor of proximity is not involved in this relationship because line II is as far from I as from III. However, as soon as the relative distances between the lines are changed, relative proximity should have *additional ordering effects;* in 12b, where the distance from II to III is smaller than the distance from II to I, proximity strengthens the grouping II-III and weakens the formation of the unit I-II. It counteracts the factor of similarity, with a resulting organization somewhat like I, II, III. In 12c, on the other hand, the distance from I to II is the smaller, and the factor of proximity therefore acts to reinforce the factor of similarity, with the result I II; III, as in the St.

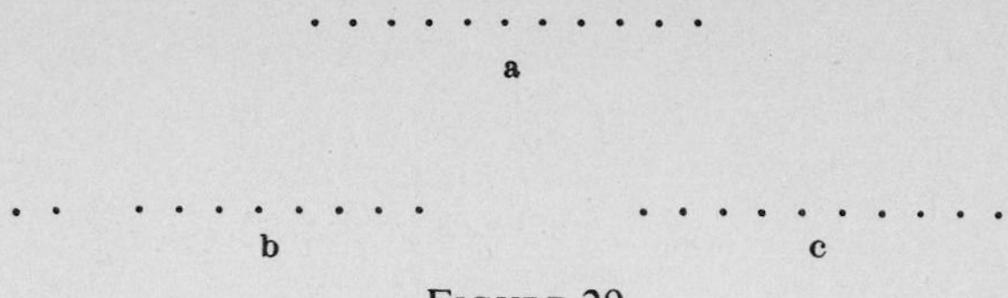

FIGURE 29

In Experiment 29 both CFs differ from the St by the absence of one single dot. In 29b, however, this dot was taken out of the interior of the line. As a consequence–according to the factor of proximity–the dots on either side of the gap are grouped into two natural parts. This subdivision is lacking in the St. But 29c, where a dot is missing from the end of the line, is just as much a single unit as the St. The experimental result is 29a $\sim$ c $\nsim$ b for 10 of 10 Os. The shortening of the line with its preservation as a unit in 29c thus decreases similarity less than the change in subdivision in 29b.

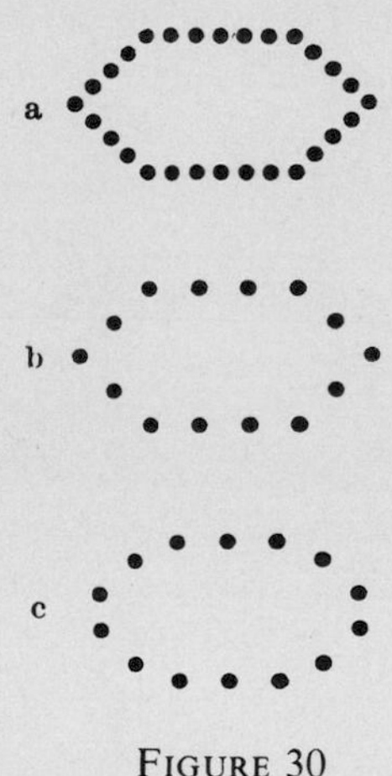

FIGURE 30

Experiment 30 has already been described in section 11. There it was shown that the result 30a $\sim$ b $\nsim$ c for 10 of 10 Os cannot be derived from either Hypothesis I or II. Here too the change, the removal of every other dot, leads to a change in the organization, in the grouping of the dots. Figure 30b, just like the St, is a polygon, a hexagon, whereas 30c is a sort of flattened elipsoid. 30b has six parts, like the St; 30c is phenomenally a continuous curve which at most is subdivided into an upper and a lower half.

Here again it is possible to test whether the differences in grouping are responsible for the result. Again the test is performed by variation of the structuring whole properties.

The more acute the angle, the more pronounced is the separation of an angulated line into two parts. Conversely, an angulated line appears more and more as a unit as the angle approaches 180° (see Rupp, 1914). As it is our contention that the difference in grouping is responsible for the result of Experiment 30, it would be expected that in figures of this type the difference between the two CFs decreases as the angles of adjoining sides become more obtuse and increases as they become more acute. These conditions are combined in Experiment 31. Figure 31a is a

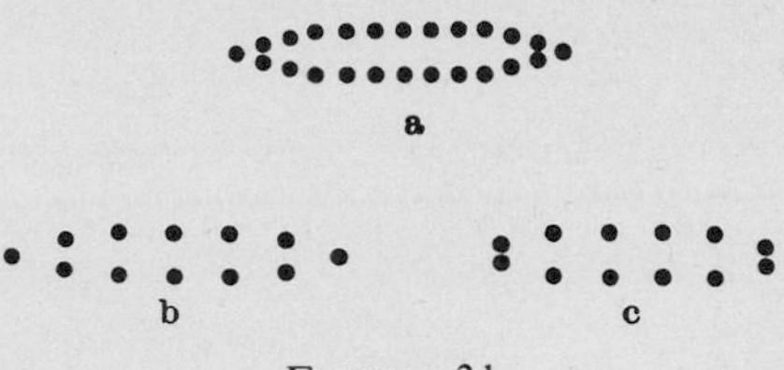

FIGURE 31

variant of 30a with two very acute and four very obtuse angles. The number of dots along each side of the St is changed in such a way that, as every other dot is omitted, either the two vertices of the acute angles drop out (31c) or the four vertices of the obtuse angles drop out (31b). In agreement with expectation, a $\sim$ b $\nsim$ c for 8 of 10 Os. The structuring effect of the obtuse angles is so small that they can be left out without noticeable change in the grouping. The reverse is true of the structuring effect of the acute angles.

The structuring effect proposed is based on the assumption that the dots along any one side form a subunit. This can be considered as proven only if the phenomenal difference in structure by itself is responsible for the results. In the case under discussion the results could be explained by other means, without taking the phenomenal structuring into account. For instance, it might be argued that the importance of dots in regions of accumulation is greater than it is in other regions. The experimental results could then be explained by the fact that the corners of dot polygons represent regions of relative accumulation. This proposition is consistent with some theories that use the principle of attention. It is best tested on figures which contain crossings. The crossing of two lines results in a relatively greater accumulation of dots than does a vertex. The point of crossing should therefore attract even more attention than a vertex. Conversely, a point of crossing–as opposed to a vertex–is no more essential to the definition of a curve than any other point, as long as the course of the lines in the region of the crossing is sufficiently determined by the remainder of their course–according to the factor of the "good curve" (Wertheimer, 1923, p. 83)–here, particularly the factor of "good continuation."

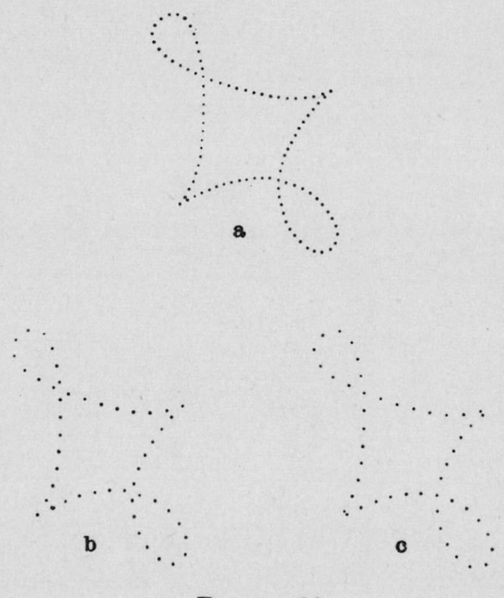

FIGURE 32

The St of Experiment 32 contains two intersections. The number of dots in each segment is so chosen that omission of every other dot leaves out either only the intersection points, as in 32b, or only the vertices, as in 32c. The result is 32a $\sim$ b $\nsim$ c for 8 of 10 Os. The intersections, then, are less important than the vertices, which have structural significance. The results prove that we are not dealing with an accumulation effect in the sense in which this concept is used in the attention theory referred to above.

It should be mentioned that a decrease in the number of dots in a line, as in 30b, 31b, 32b, is known to decrease the stability of structuring. "If a constellation contains fewer dots the result is . . . no longer as compelling, the situation in general altogether more labile" (Wertheimer, 1923, p. 73). In our experiments, however, this factor is important only in Figures 31b and c, where a subject occasionally sees, rather than the grouping as in the St, a constellation in which dot pairs situated one above the other are grouped together. This grouping, however, is "not as good." The structuring of 31b, which is the same as that of the St, is preferred.

The last experiments were so arranged that the grouping of the St was entirely preserved in one of the CFs. They show that, everything else being equal, *the variant which preserves the grouping is more similar to the St.* [1]

27. CHANGE OF GROUPING IN ALL COMPARISON FIGURES

If the grouping of the parts is not preserved in either of the CFs the different degrees of change may permit conclusions about similarity. In Experiment 33, 12 lines of equal length make up the St; in each CF, 6 lines have been removed, so that in numbers the change is the same in all three CFs. But in grouping

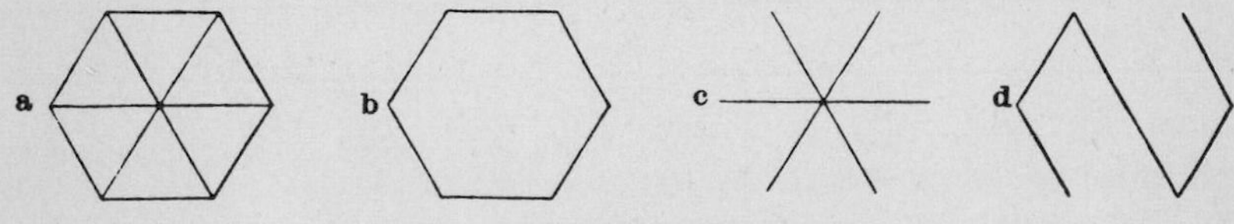

FIGURE 33

the situations are far from equal. In the St, 6 lines form the "outline" and the other 6 form the "inner star." The lines remaining in 33b and c are grouped in the same way as in the St. But in

[1] [Our interpretation of Experiments 29, 30, 31, and 32 is that the presence or absence of some corners, vertices, line segments, etc., changes the structure, the whole qualities, the "phenomenal picture," and this in turn influences similarity.

During the 1950s the role played by corners, intersections (Hochberg and McAlister, 1953), and points of sharp curvature (Attneave, 1954) was again examined. The investigators hoped to reduce whole qualities, structure, and Gestalt factors to quantitative, information-theoretical statements about vertices, line segments, and points of maximal curvature, the reverse of the position taken here.

This is not the place for a critical review of Attneave's and Hochberg's efforts, except to suggest that Experiments 29, 30, 31, and 32 in no way support their views. In my opinion, the reduction attempted by these information theorists was unsuccessful. However, later efforts to apply information theory, by Garner and co-workers (e.g., Handel and Garner, 1966), are compatible with the Gestalt point of view.—E.G.]

33d three new groupings are formed, each consisting of two lines: the two central lines are completely merged into one, and the four outer ones are related to each other in pairs, as two "couples." None of these relations are present in this way in the St. The experimental results, in order of decreasing similarity, are 33b, c, d for 9 of 10 Os; 1 O chooses the order b, d, c.

The position of 33d in this series corresponds to the difference in grouping; the rank order of b and c, on the other hand, does not follow from the differences in grouping alone. Here consideration of further structural determinants is necessary (see section 28).

B. Changes of Phenomenal Function of the Parts in the Whole and Change of Grouping

28. Similarity of the "more function-preserving" variant

The "parts" which phenomenally result from the particular kind of grouping are phenomenally defined by their function. In a structured whole the parts are experienced not in isolation but as *having a specific function within the whole.* Any change in the structure leads to a change in the function of parts as well.[2] Changes of structure are not completely defined as phenomenal changes unless the functions of the parts are taken into consideration. Therefore the investigation of grouping needs to be supplemented in this respect.

For the main points, lines, and groups of lines of 33a, b, c, d, for instance, the following is a comparison of the functions of the parts.

In 33a all the corner points are homologous.[3] The same is true in 33b. In 33d two former corner points are "end points," two form the "middle of the wing," two are "starting points" of the wings and at the same time "end points" of the straight line in the middle. Both a and c have a center which is the "origin of the star" and also represents the "phenomenal center" of the figure. In 33b, too, where an actual center is missing, the "phe-

[2] This matter is discussed in detail elsewhere. See especially Wertheimer (1933, pp. 353f.); also Ternus (1926) and Kopfermann (1930).

[3] The differences in orientation in space cause small differences of function. These can, however, be neglected in first approximation.

nomenal center" is still in this location. In d the center is not emphasized even to this extent. In a and b the outer edges form the "contour," and are homologous to each other as parts of equal weight[4] in the contour. The interior lines in a and the lines in c are likewise homologous as "rays." Together they form the "inner figure" or "interior detail." In d four parts of the "contour" are connected to two parts of the "inner figure" to form a new unit with three subunits, two "wings" asymmetrically connected by an "oblique center line." The "oblique center line" of d is a unit, whereas in a the same lines–considered as separate pieces–form two of the six "radii."[5] In summary, those parts which are retained in b and c have the same functional relations as in the St 33a; they are homologous. Furthermore, they are contained in the St as true parts, 33b as "contour," 33c as "inner figure." Figure 33d is not contained phenomenally in the St at all for most observers. (The reader may convince himself of this by intentionally trying to visualize the lines of 33d in 33a simultaneously as a unit.) The functions are now found to have a rank order that matches the rank order found above for the grouping. In addition, it is now possible to interpret the greater similarity to the St of 33b compared to 33c. The function of "contour" is *more essential* for the phenomenal appearance than is that of "inner detail." One function is *phenomenally subordinate* to the other. This is reflected in their relevance for similarity.

It should particularly be noted that in this case consideration of grouping *alone* was not enough to derive the degree of similarity.

29. FUNCTION AND FUNCTION CARRIER: CONSTANCY OF STRUCTURE AS PRESERVATION OF FUNCTIONS

We now ask, what happens to a function whose carrier is removed or changed?

In Experiment 30, when the corner dots are removed (30c) their function also disappears; conversely, when the corner dots are preserved (30b) the figure has "corners." In this example, then, the function and its bearer are linked to each other.

[4] See footnote 3.

[5] See the analysis of the same figure in Kopfermann (1930, p. 329). There the same considerations prove to be informative for the question of three-dimensional perception.

In Experiment 9, when the shorter rays are lengthened (9b), their function is also changed. Now they are homologous to the other group of rays, and their function is the same as that of the other group; they are now "material of a star with equal rays."

In Figure 10b the shift in position of the dots creates new functions for them: they become the corners of a square.

In the cases listed, with the omission of or change in the carrier, its function is likewise omitted, or changed as in 30c, the corners in 10b, the short rays in 9b. And, conversely, as in 30b, when the carrier is preserved, the function is preserved independent of other changes of the figure.

However, this is not true in general. Even in Experiments 9 and 10 it is apparent that the changes made in the CFs lead to changes of function in those parts of the figure *which are not directly changed* as well.

In 9b the unchanged rays, which were "long" in the St, are no longer a "long system of rays" with a separate function.

In 10b the unchanged dots undergo a change of function. From being equivalent "points on the periphery of a circle" or "corners of an octagon" they are transformed into "centers of edges" which are "subordinate" to the new corners.

In Figure 33d also, the functions of the unchanged parts are modified, as was shown above.

These cases demonstrate that function and carrier of function can vary independently of each other. The function can change without change of the carrier.

Finally, the *function* may be undisturbed even though its *carrier* is disturbed or eliminated.

In Experiment 29 the last dot has the function of "end point." If it is dropped, as in 29c, the function remains; the next dot becomes the end point.

In Figure 1a the lowest row of dots is the "lower contour." If the carrier of this function is removed, as in 1b and c, the function is preserved; it is transferred to a new carrier.

In Figure 10a all the dots are homologous "points on the periphery." In 10c they are all shifted but their function is preserved.

In all these examples, those figures in which function is conserved are the more similar, *regardless of whether its original carrier appears exactly as in the St and even if the original carrier does not appear at all.*

If we generalize the meaning of the term structure to include the grouping of the parts *and* their function, the result can be formulated as follows. *The variant which, everything else being equal, best conserves the structure is the more similar.*

30. ONLY INDIVIDUAL FUNCTIONS CAN BE RELATED AS HOMOLOGUES

The consideration of function instead of the carriers of function solves the previous difficulties with homology. For Experiment 11 the possibility of assigning homology according to function was already suggested in section 10. For cases in which an individual or form function is carried by one or more material elements, however, the problem is somewhat more complicated.

In Experiment 29, when the end point was removed in 29c the "end point" function was transferred to the next dot. Where, then, is *its* previous function, the function of the "next to last dot"? (And correspondingly of the following dots.) Obviously the dots cannot be matched up in this way; the function of one of them would be missing. Now phenomenally there is certainly no evidence of this. Phenomenally, 29c is a variant with all the structural homologues, in the sense that all the functions of the St are represented. It is therefore necessary to distinguish between the *material function,* which is assigned to all the dots as elements of a larger entity, and the form or *individual functions,* which some particular elements have by virtue of their special position within the whole. Only the first and the last dots in 29a have well-defined individual functions. They are distinguished as "ends" by their positions. The functions of "next to last," "second from last," etc., do not exist phenomenally, if an optimal impression of material has been achieved.

This is true even though it is possible to realize phenomenally the next to the last dot as such: this function is only *derived* from the *direct* form function of the "last," as suggested by the expression "last but one." The possibility of individual phenomenal realization decreases very quickly: the phenomenal realization of the "81st dot from the last" as such is impossible. Such a function does not exist even as a derived function. Likewise it is impossible to realize simultaneously individual functions for all the dots in the *entire* row in 29a.

One might, distrusting intuition, still suspect such functions, and hypothesize that the lack of homology of the dots is "overlooked" by mistake; that the dots might be "mistaken for each other" because of their similarity and equal arrangement. This hypothesis corresponds to the "unnoticed sensations" postulated by earlier psychologists. Such a complication of the theory–the assumption of functions which are, however, then not noticed–makes sense only if it is possible to point to facts which require it (see Köhler, 1913)–if, for instance, the alleged material functions emerge and affect similarity as soon as the material elements are no longer "equal" and thus no longer "subject to being mistaken for one another." Experiment 1 represents such a case. The elements of 1a are dotted lines, and they are clearly of *different* lengths. Nevertheless the functions are conserved in the transition from 1a to 1b to 1c. In this process the corner function passes to geometrically equal carriers while the contour function passes to different carriers (i.e., carriers of different lengths).[6]

Thus we distinguish an unindividualized "material function" of a group of elements from an individualized form function of some elements and larger parts determined by their position and by the over-all arrangement.

31. CASES OF INDIVIDUAL FUNCTIONS FOR THE PART, MATERIAL FUNCTION FOR THE WHOLE

The material elements derive individual functions from their position within the whole–"end point" in 29, "contour" in 1. Individual functions, however, may arise in still another context, if the material elements are themselves composed of parts. These functions, derived from the organization of the material elements, are also individual ones. Therefore *the requirement that they be conserved in a variant which conserves structure again applies.* For instance, in Figure 34a the elements consist of "pairs"

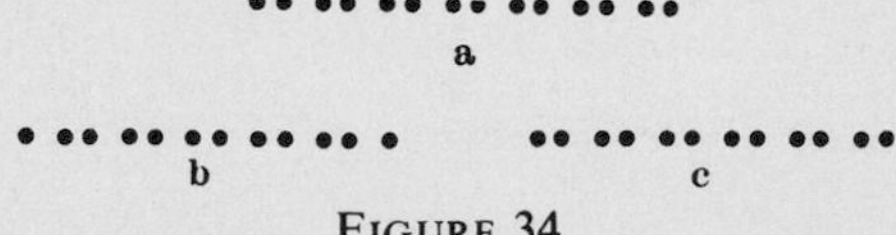

FIGURE 34

[6] Ternus (1926, p. 159) reported parallel results for the phenomenal identity of geometrically unequal figural features. In his experiments too, unequal subwholes were found to be identical on the basis of having the same function, without the parts being homologous to each other on an individual matching basis.

of dots. As material elements the "pairs" have no individual function. If a pair is removed, as in 34c, the same considerations apply for the pairs which were found to apply in 29c for the dots. The "end" function is shifted. Within the pairs, however, there exist further functions which are derived from the structure of the elementary pair, the function of "partners." These functions are individualized because each pair—unlike the dotted line in 1a—consists of only two relatively large dots, and is separated from adjoining pairs by a distance that is large compared to the size of the pair. If, on the other hand, the two outermost dots of the St are removed, as in 34b, two pairs are each short a "partner." Accordingly, the result is 34a $\sim$ c $\not\sim$ b for 9 of 10 Os.[7]

Experiment 35, a modification of Experiment 1, has analogous

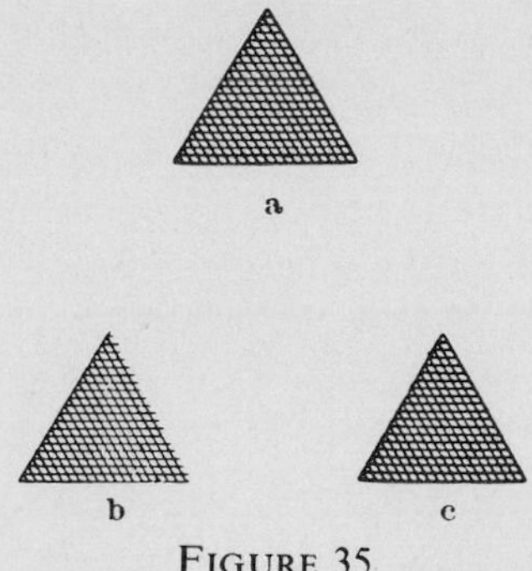

FIGURE 35

results. In 35c, removal of the unindividualized entire element-row of rhombi makes possible a transfer of function. The next row as a whole becomes the "margin" row; the individual rhombi have no homologues. If, however, only the outside line is removed—which, geometrically speaking, means "less"—the individual functions within the material elements are destroyed. The "rhombi" of the border row in 35a and c become "parallel hatchings" in 35b. Accordingly, 35a $\sim$ c $\not\sim$ b for 8 of 10 Os.

Finally, here too Rule 2 applies. With relatively few and large elements the phenomenal separation into a hierarchy of material systems disappears in the phenomenal organization. This is

[7] Because of the principle of proximity (Wertheimer, 1923), organization of 34b into equal pairs with a *large* interior distance does not occur and therefore need not be discussed.

shown in Figure 36a, a segment of 35a. Here the outer line has individual functions not only for individual rhombi but for the entire figure. Consequently, when the same changes are made as

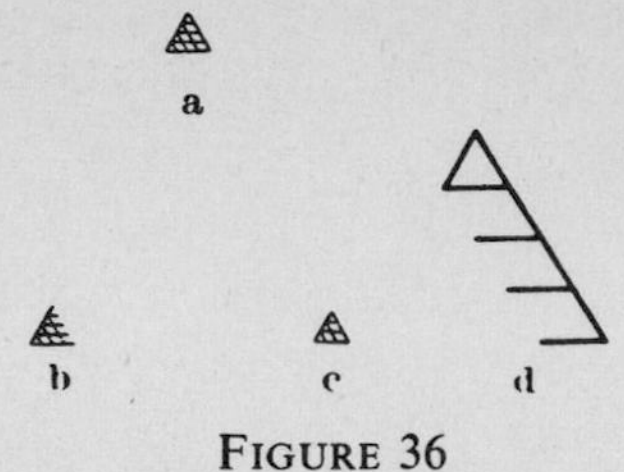

FIGURE 36

in the CFs of Experiment 35, neither of the variants conserves the structure with complete fidelity. But the structure of 36b is closer to the St than that of 36c. It is easy to complete 36b to make 36a. The parts have the same function as in 36a; only "one line is missing" which exists in the St too as a "unit," as a true part, as "border." Figure 36b appears as 36a with a "defect." 36c, on the other hand, is a *completed* figure in itself. While in 36b there is a "vector force directed toward completion" (toward the St), 36c does not "require" enlargement or completion. Its completion to the St would require the complicated addition of 36d which as such, in this grouping, is not phenomenally contained in the St. The structure of 35c is noticeably simpler than that of 36a. Accordingly, the results of Experiment 36 are a $\sim$ b $\not\sim$ c for 8 of 10 Os. The experiment shows that a true *change of structure* decreases similarity more than even a considerable *"defect" without changes in the grouping and the functions of the remainder.*

5

SIMILARITY IN DISTORTION: *PRÄGNANZ*

32. DISTINCTION BETWEEN DISTORTION AND CHANGE OF GROUPING

With respect to changes in grouping it has been shown that similarity depends on the agreement of those qualities which determine the phenomenal organization. In the following experiments, cases were examined in which the change does not go as far as to destroy the grouping. Here the figure is merely *distorted.*

The following example may clarify the distinction between change of organization and distortion. An angle (abg in Figure 37) changes slowly by a continuous movement of the line bg to

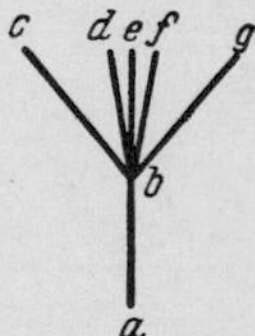

FIGURE 37

the left so that the angle abg goes through the stages abf, abe, abd (Figure 37), etc. [1] Then one sees that in the stages g to f and d to c the angle first increases in size and then decreases again. In the stage f to d, however, during which the two lines of the "angle" should become the undivided "straight line" abe, one sees an angle of constant magnitude which turns out of the plane of projection free in space.

[1] To produce this change let a constant angle made of wire like abg rotate about the line ab and observe the shadow of this structure. The shadow changes as described in the text. See Metzger (1934).

The change in angulation is a distortion; the transition into a straight line, abe, would be a change in structure, a change in grouping, and a change in functions. This experiment shows, moreover, that the distinction is relevant beyond problems of similarity.

33. MAIN EXPERIMENTS ON DISTORTION

First a few examples of such distortion. Most of these experiments cannot be explained by Hypothesis I or II. However, the reasons will no longer be discussed in detail.

In both CFs of Figure 38, the dots have been shifted by approximately equal amounts, in 38b so that the verticals are tilted slightly in an oblique direction, in 38c so that only the positions of the dots on the vertical lines are changed. The result is 38a $\sim$ c $\not\sim$ b for 18 of 20 Os. [2]

In Experiment 39 the St, 39a, is symmetrical. CF 39b is identi-

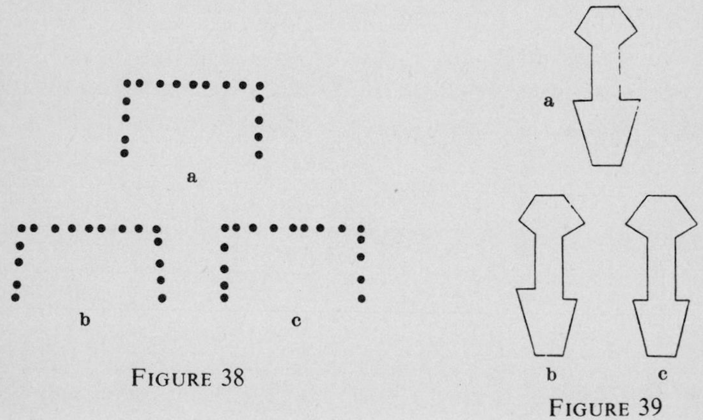

FIGURE 38

FIGURE 39

cal with the St on the left side; the right side is distorted by changes in the distances as well as in the angles. In CF 39c both sides are distorted from the St, in such a way that the right side is the same as that of 39b, and the left side is its mirror image. CF 39c is thus changed more than 39b, but it is symmetrical like

[2] See section 12. In the actual figures used the sum of the shifts—regardless of the direction of shift—in 38b was about 26 mm., in 38c about 28 mm. The small difference thus favors 38b. It may be disregarded all the more since the amounts of shift here and in the control Experiments 43 and 44 are the same, so that any possible advantage of one variant over the other would influence all results in the same direction.

the St. Conservation of symmetry outweighs the greater changes in distances and angles: 39a $\sim$ c $\nsim$ b for 10 of 10 Os.

In 40a the teeth form a straight contour line. This regularity is

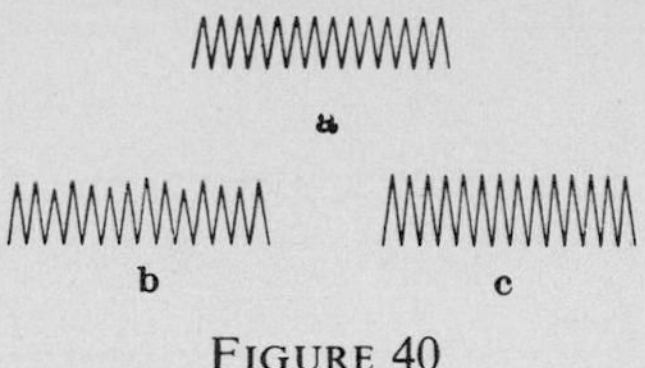

FIGURE 40

conserved in c, and destroyed in b. The changes in distances and angles, however, are greater in c than in b. Regularity is the more sensitive quality: the result is 40a $\sim$ c $\nsim$ b for 11 of 11 Os.

Figure 41a consists of two obtuse angles, one above the other.

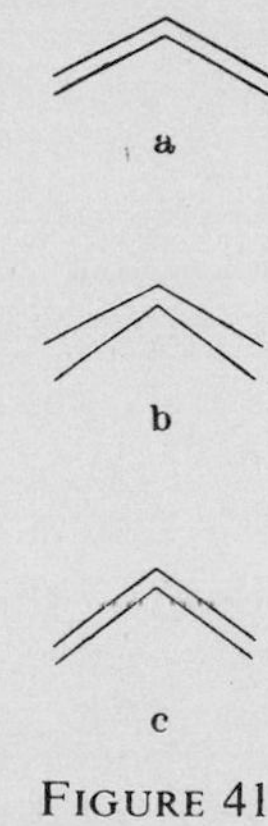

FIGURE 41

In CF 41b the upper angle is unchanged, the lower one decreased from 120° to 105°. This disturbs the parallelity of the lines. In CF 41c both angles are decreased to 105°, so the two lines are again parallel. The result is very definitely 41a $\sim$ c $\nsim$ b. Here, then, "parallelity" is more sensitive to change than are the absolute values of the angles. It should be stated parenthetically that this would not hold in certain special cases, for instance for angles of 90° and perpendicular orientation of one pair of lines.

In Experiment 42 the St, 42a, consists of a straight line and a circular arc of a certain height. In CF 42b, the height of the arc, and therefore the over-all height—"thickness"—of the figure, is

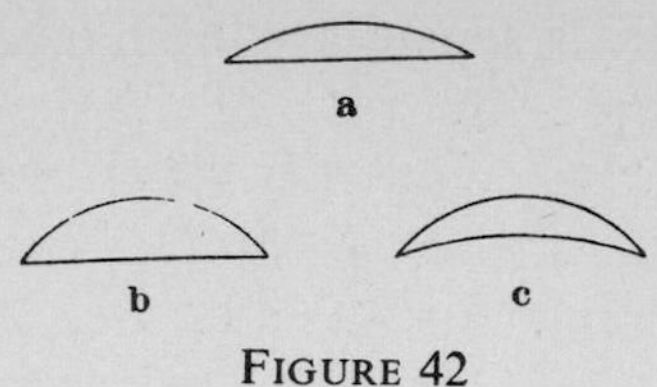

FIGURE 42

increased by ⅔. In CF 42c, the lower line is likewise a circular arc so that both lines are curved. The curvature of the upper line is the same as in 42b; that of the lower line is adjusted so that in "over-all thickness" the figure is the same as the St. The results were a $\sim$ b $\not\sim$ c for 11 of 12 Os. Here the rectilinearity of the lower border is more sensitive to change than the "thickness" of the figure.

34. INTERPRETATION OF THE RESULTS

These experiments merely show that of the qualities changed, one is more sensitive to change than the other. Furthermore, they show that degrees of similarity do not simply correspond to the amount of change in arbitrary pieces (as opposed to true components) or proportions. For instance, Experiment 39 shows that the constellation of positions and measurements of *one side of the figure as a unit in relation to the other* is more sensitive to change than is the constellation of the *parts of one or both sides* among themselves. Experiment 42 shows that the curvature of *one* line is more sensitive to change than the measurements which define the "thickness" of the figure.

One might assume that the *geometrical qualities* concerned *in themselves* are more effective—that, for example, in Figure 40 the ratio or the difference or another mathematical function of (relation between) the sizes of the teeth are more effective *under all conditions, no matter what the value of this function is,* than, say, a mathematical relation between the height and the width of the teeth or a relation between the absolute values or magnitudes of the measurements. Such reasoning, even though it would require further experimental elaboration, would at least be compatible with the experiments described so far.

But there is another possibility, namely that it is *just the particular value* of the effective entity in the cases under discussion that is responsible for its sensitivity to change: that—again using Figure 40 as an example—the ratio of the heights of the teeth in itself is not particularly sensitive but that the sensitivity hinges on the particular value of the ratio, namely the ratio of 1/1; that the relationship between the heights of the teeth is not governing in general but only in the case of *just this particular value of the ratio.* And similarly, in Experiment 39, that it is not a constellation of homologues in general that is decisive but only in the *singular case of a symmetrical constellation.* And the other examples could be explained in analogous ways.

This second interpretation of the results leads directly to the principle of selection of the qualities from the point of view of *phenomenal reality,* which has been successful on previous occasions. For the phenomenal impression, the rule applies that

> . . . if a piece of the stimulus configuration is varied systematically step by step, the resulting impressions are psychologically not a set of individually characteristic impressions of equal weight, changing in corresponding steps; rather, the result shows certain "steps of *prägnanz*" with their "ranges." The course shows "discontinuities." Intermediate steps typically appear "in the sense of one of the *prägnanz* forms" [Wertheimer, 1923, p. 319].

Among the many values which a geometrical variable can assume there are a few, the *"prägnant"* ones, which are singled out. Psychologically, they are realized with preference. Phenomenally, 40a and b are composed not of teeth whose ratio in a has the value 1 and in b has another, equally realized value, ≠ 1. Rather, in a the teeth appear as *singularly* "equal," their arrangement as *singularly* "regular," whereas in b there is phenomenally no positive characterization of the value of the *nonsingular* ratio. The teeth merely appear to be, in a negative way, "unequal" and "irregular." Corresponding explanations can be given for parallelity in Experiment 41, for symmetry in 39, for perpendicularity in 38, and for rectilinearity in 42. In all these cases the quality which is sensitive to change is *prägnant* or, as we shall say, *singular,* [3] and

[3] [It has been customary to leave the German words *Prägnanz* and *prägnant* untranslated. I propose here to use the terms *singularity* and *singular* as English equivalents. When a trait is called singular this should be understood as a shortened expression for a singular value of the trait. If parallelity is called singular, this is to say that among possible values for divergence of two lines the value of zero degrees is a singular one, distinguished as parallelity.—E.G.]

phenomenally realized as the individually characteristic quality.

The reverse is true of the values of those qualities which proved to be less sensitive to change in the experiments. The changed individual distances, angles, ratios, and proportions in Figure 39 are perceived not as "*exactly* these" but rather as "*approximately* these." The phenomenal impression of these attributes corresponds to *a range of possible values only approximately defined.* The same thing is true in Figure 40 of the absolute height of the teeth, of the ratio between the height and the width, and of the ratio between the height and the total length of the figure; in Figure 38 of the arrangement of the dots along the lines; and in Figure 41 of the size of each of the two angles taken separately.

There is, then, a positive correlation between attributes of *singular value* and *sensitivity to change* on the one hand, and between the *range character* of an attribute and its *insensitivity* to change on the other. It is, then, very probable that conservation of *singular values of geometrical parameters* is the basis of the similarity of the CF in which a particular attribute is unchanged. Not only is it probable, it can easily be tested experimentally. All that is needed are control experiments in which figures like those investigated above are used with different values for the attributes in question, singular ones instead of nonsingular, and vice versa.

35. CONTROL EXPERIMENTS

If in the control experiments an originally singular quality is made nonsingular or an originally nonsingular quality is made singular, then all one can expect, according to the concepts developed here, is that the variant corresponding to the originally similar variant will lose in similarity. How large this loss will be, if it will lead to equal similarity or even to reversal in the relative similarities, cannot be predicted. In this respect only the experiments themselves will give definite information.

Figure 43 is a control experiment for Experiment 38. The nonsingular arrangement of the dots in 38a is here replaced by a singular arrangement. The two CFs are varied in exactly the same way as are 38b and c. In 43c the dots are shifted in the same direction and by the same amount as in 38c, in 43b the

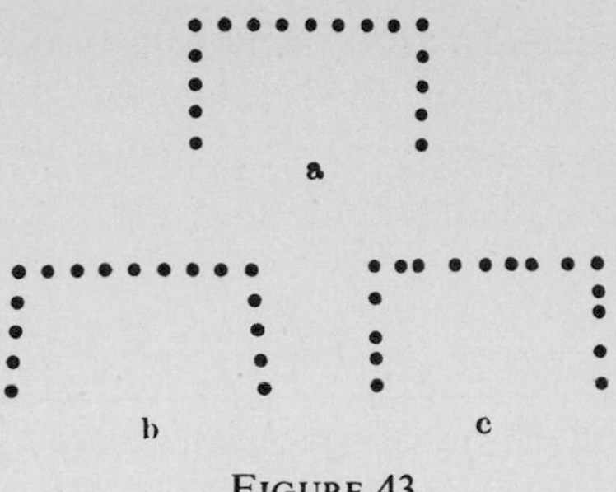

FIGURE 43

verticals are turned by the same amount as in 38b. Now a singular attribute is disturbed in *both* CFs, and the decision between them is very difficult: 10 of 20 Os chose b, 10 chose c. It is only when the distribution of the dots is nonsingular, then, that changes in the positions of the dots on the lines are less important than disturbance of the right angles. *If distribution of the dots too is singular, the two changes are equivalent.*

In a second control for Experiment 38, the distribution of the dots was again singular but the singular right angles were replaced by nonsingular acute angles of 75° (see Figure 44a). The

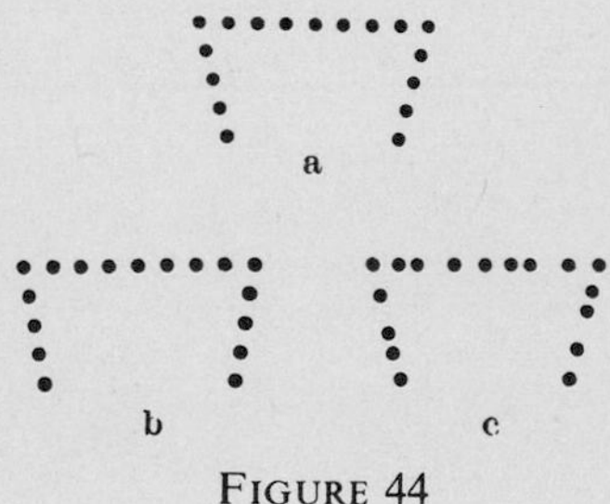

FIGURE 44

two CFs are varied in the same way as are the CFs in Experiments 38 and 43, resulting in CFs 44b and c. Now the decision is again unequivocal, between a singular quality–distribution of dots–and a nonsingular quality–angle. The result is 44a $\sim$ b $\not\sim$ c for 9 of 10 Os, as expected.

The controls for Experiments 39, 40, 41, and 42 were so designed that only the attribute which was originally singular was made *nonsingular too.* Here, then, as indicated above, it is not expected that the results will be a complete reversal of the results of the main experiment. The controls are shown in Figures 45, 46, 47, and 48.

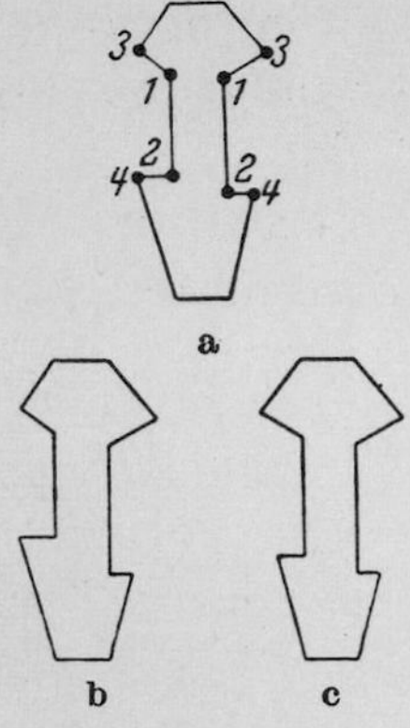

FIGURE 45

Description: 45b is identical with 45a in its left half. On the right side points 1 and 2 are shifted downward, point 3 outward, point 4 closer to the middle.

45c is not identical with 45a on either side. Its right half is identical with the right half of 45b. On the left side points 1 and 2 are shifted downward, point 3 outward, point 4 closer to the middle with respect to the corresponding points of 45b.

Details of Experiments 45, 46, 47, 48. In Figure 45 the St is the same as 39b. CF 45b again, as in the previous experiment, shares the left side with the St 45a, the right side being changed in relation to the left by about the same amount as 39b is changed in relation to 39a. In 45c *both* sides are changed in this way, so that the distances between homologous points 1 and 1, 2 and 2 (see Figure 45a) are the same in a and c. Of 10 Os 5 chose b and 5 c.

In Experiment 46, the control for Experiment 40, the teeth in

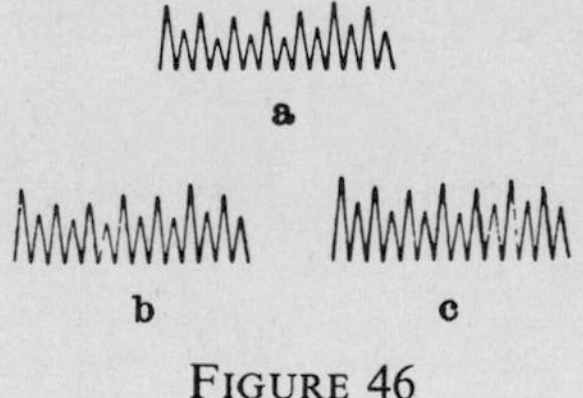

FIGURE 46

the St 46a are already nonsingularly *unequal;* the upper ends of the teeth form not a straight line but an irregular one.

As in 40b, these points were raised in 46b by various small amounts (2-7 mm. in the actual drawing); in 46c they were raised by an *equal* and larger amount (10 mm. in the actual drawing). Thus in c the *relative* positions of the points in relation *to one another* are the same as in the St, whereas in b the distances *from the base line* deviate less from the corresponding values of the St. Both changes, however, give rise to such small phenomenal changes in the whole that the choice between the CFs is very difficult. One O sees no difference at all in the similarity of the two variants, 6 judge a ∼ b ≁ c, and 4 judge the reverse. Thus the result is a ∼ b ≁ c for 6.5 of 11 Os.

In Experiment 47, the control for 41, the two lines in the St are now not parallel. Starting from this St, the variations are like

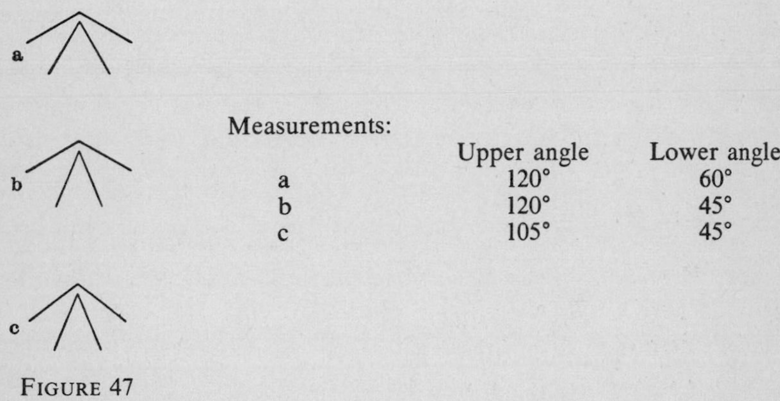

Measurements:

	Upper angle	Lower angle
a	120°	60°
b	120°	45°
c	105°	45°

FIGURE 47

those in Experiment 41: in 47b the upper angle is the same as in the St; in 47c both angles are decreased by 15°. As the "parallelity" of the lines in the St is preserved in 41c, so the degree of "divergence" of the lines in the St is conserved in 47c. Agreement in the divergence, now nonsingular, is, however, much less effective in determining relative similarity than is agreement in parallelity: the piecemeal agreement between a and b, in the angle of the upper lines, is now decisive–47a ∼ b ≁ c for 8 of 10 Os.

The St of Experiment 48, the control for 42, is the same as 42c. Now both lines of the St are nonsingularly "curved." Further variations were the same as in Experiment 42: in 48b the lower

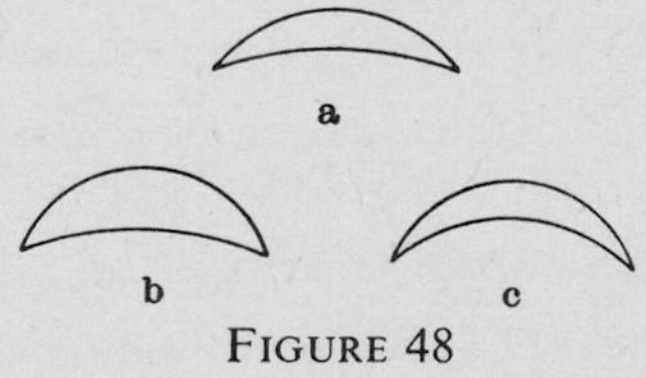

FIGURE 48

line is unchanged, the upper line is more curved, and the thickness (= difference in the height of the arc) is thus increased. In 48c the upper line is the same as that of 48b, and the lower line is more curved. Neither line is the same as in the St; a and c agree, however, in thickness, as did 42a and c. This quality of the whole now seems to be of relatively greater phenomenal reality: for 8 of 12 Os 48a $\sim$ c $\nsim$ b, the reverse of the results of Experiment 42.

These control experiments show the expected decrease in similarity of the variant whose corresponding variant was preferred in the original experiment. Reversing the singularity relationships in Experiment 44 causes a reversal of similarity; removing the difference in singularity leads to approximately equal similarity in Experiments 43, 45, and 46, and even to a reversal of similarity in Experiments 47 and 48.

It is thus confirmed that *singular values, being phenomenally most strongly realized, also have maximum effects for similarity.*

36. ON REALIZATION OF NONSINGULAR VALUES

For the control experiments in which the figures contain only *non*singular qualities, 45, 46, 47, and 48, we must assume that the results are likewise based on differences in the degree of phenomenal realization of the two attributes in question. Thus we must assume that nonsingular values of qualities differ *among themselves* in the degree to which they are phenomenally realized, even though such differences will be smaller than the difference between a singular and a nonsingular value. Only this assumption can explain the fact that variations in the nonsingular range of a feature of a figure produce differences in similarity, although not as marked ones. For instance, a slightly different version of Figure 28 (where the variations were also of two nonsingular features, the sizes of the dots and the ratio between the two sizes), in which the nonsingular ratio between the dots was somewhat closer to the singular "equality" than in the figure illustrated, yielded approximately equal similarity of the two variants: a $\sim$ b $\nsim$ c for 4.5 of 8 Os, as against 7 of 8 Os in the version shown. It is not possible to test this interpretation of these nonsingular values within the scope of this investigation. Testing would require systematic examination of individual features such as, in Experiment 48, "thickness," "individual curvature," and "total curvature," and similarly in the other experiments. At any rate, it seems certain that there are considerable differences in the degree of realization of nonsingular values, on the basis of investigations by Schneider (1932, p. 585). That the effects of the differences found by Schneider are partly in a different direction than those found here is due to the fact that his experiments used variations in the threshold region, his material contained figures of a different type, and, finally, he used only *one* very special type of variation.

37. THE MEANING OF "REALIZATION"

The general principle for explaining these findings is the following. We assume that of all the geometrical parameters, measurements, and relationships present or conceivable in a figure, only a few are phenomenally "given" or "realized." This should not be taken to mean that all the other properties are completely irrelevant for the phenomenal picture and for similarity–that, for instance, "curvature" in Experiment 48, being nonsingular, does not exist phenomenally. Obviously the curvature is experienced, but a small change in the nonsingular curvature corresponds to *almost no* phenomenal difference, whereas the same change applied to a singular starting value, "curvature zero," may result in a very marked phenomenal change. That is, in the nonsingular case the *particular value* of curvature is not realized as such, and a more or less *extended range* of neighboring values will yield nearly the same phenomenal experience of curvature.

Furthermore, to say that the value of "curvature zero" is singular and therefore "realized" does not imply that the straight line appears phenomenally as a "curve of curvature zero," but that the *specific characteristic experience* of "straightness" corresponds to this particular singular value. Similarly, in Experiment 40 the particular proportion 1/1 is not experienced as a proportion of value 1; rather, it is experienced as the phenomenally distinguished "equality" of the teeth or "regularity" of the comb formed by them. This and only this is intended by the term "realized."

38. SIMILARITY OF NONSINGULAR VARIANTS IN DIFFERENT SINGULARITY REGIONS

Variation of a geometrical parameter up to a singular value and then beyond this value results, in general, in three kinds of phenomenal impression: first and second, the nonsingular impressions of the variants on either side of the singular value, which may be quite similar to each other; and third, the qualitatively different impression of the singular variant.

This phenomenon was illustrated in section 32 by Metzger's (1934) experiment. Another example is furnished by Experiment 6. The St, 6a, and CF 6b both show a certain "roundness"–in 6b only poorly represented; it could be made more striking by using more dots or full lines. In 6c, on the other side of the singular value, there is a kind of *"pointedness."* In between b and c lies the singular figure, a *"square."*

As a rule, these three groups of impressions are independent. No experimental information is available about their phenomenal relationships. Therefore we have not investigated the similarity relations among such configurations.[4]

But in other cases the situation is quite different: often the nonsingular variants on *both* sides of the singular value are extraordinarily similar. It is not possible to formulate in general what the conditions are for such an occurrence. However, it is easily demonstrated in particular instances, and the conditions for the phenomenon are then readily ascertained. In Experiment 9, for instance, with gradual increase of the short rays only the singular appearance of the "star with equal rays" stands out. But the impressions of the variants on either side of this singular value are no more different from each other than are those on one side among themselves. This is true at least for a fairly large range of variation in the length of the short rays. In this instance the phenomenon depends mainly on the irrelevance of the direction in space of the individual rays, as already discussed in section 23. Similarly, in Experiment 11, where the "parallelity" of all three lines (11b) is singular, the nonsingular impressions on either side of it are nearly equivalent.

A rule of thumb for such cases would be that the nonsingular is more similar to the nonsingular than to the singular. This rule

[4] [I have recently studied this subject experimentally. The findings are reported in Chapter 7 of this monograph.–E.G.]

will not be discussed further, since its range of application cannot yet be delimited. [5]

39. SIMILARITY AS AGREEMENT IN PHENOMENALLY REALIZED QUALITIES

Similarity is based on the degree of agreement of the phenomenal grouping and other phenomenally realized qualities. Grouping and realized qualities make up what I am calling the "phenomenal picture." Our results can then be expressed in the general statement that *the similarity of two figures depends on the agreement of their phenomenal pictures.* This formulation is empty, to be sure, compared with our concrete findings. However, it allows some basic conclusions and remarks related to our results.

1. *Relation to Hypotheses I and II.* In Hypotheses I and II similarity is related to changes in certain sets of *geometrical characteristics of the objects.* In contrast, the present statement does not posit yet a third set of geometrical characteristics as the basis for the experience of similarity. Rather, it relates differences in similarity to differences in the phenomenal pictures. In many instances, however, the changes in the phenomenal picture happen to correspond exactly to the geometrical changes with which Hypothesis I or II deals. These are cases such as those in Chapters 1 and 2 that were mentioned as compatible with Hypothesis I or II; and also, for Hypothesis II, the cases in Chapter 3 in which there was *no separation* into material and form, e.g., Experiments 10, 21, and 25. The two hypotheses are, then, not refuted but only restricted to certain types of variations. They apply within the domain in which the phenomenal picture is varied in conformity with them. A detailed delineation of the domain within which each of the two hypotheses applies will not be undertaken here. Some of the conditions required for their valid application can be derived directly from our results so far.

2. *The qualities that determine the phenomenal picture.* On the other hand, the experiments, particularly those related to singularity, show that these hypotheses cannot be amended to furnish *generally valid* explanations by invoking "higher-order relations." It is clear that, for example, the qualities of the "dot constellation" in Figure 38 are described by a mathematical expression *of*

[5] [This has become the subject of Chapter 7.—E.G.]

the same order as that which describes the qualities of the dot constellations in Figures 43 and 44. The decision about similarity depends not on the *order* of the mathematical expression, which must be the same in all three figures, but on the particular value of the expression in the individual figures. We are unable to offer an explicit formula to specify in every possible case which values are singular; it is possible only to determine them empirically in each case. Proponents of stimulus formulas would be similarly hard put to designate concretely, in a particular case, the required proportions or "higher-order relations," let alone supply a general formula for this purpose. As far as I know, no attempt to demonstrate the relevant relations concretely has ever been made.[6]

Still, reliance on relations, typified by Hypothesis II, is based on the insight, which was confirmed here, that the phenomenal qualities which are relevant for similarity are essentially *whole qualities* of the design under consideration. But it must be added that these qualities are not completely characterized merely as

[6] [Gestalt theory has often been accused of vagueness in the definition of key concepts such as, in this case, singularity *(Prägnanz)*. In the text the argument is advanced that rival theories are equally unable to specify operationally which "parts" or "pieces" (Hypothesis I) or "relations" (Hypothesis II) are responsible for experienced similarity.

I would like to refute this accusation at a more fundamental level. The situation is one frequently encountered in physics, for example, in the theory of radiation. In 1916, combining experimental evidence with thermodynamic reasoning, Einstein defined the so-called Einstein Coefficients. They still form the basis of the theory of absorption and emission of radiation. At the time of Einstein's publication nobody knew how to calculate these coefficients; they had to be determined experimentally. It took more than a decade to develop the theory which made it possible to calculate these coefficients, at least *in principle*; but even now, with the aid of computers, most coefficients can only be calculated approximately.

The situation is the same in respect to the concept of singularity. The early Gestalt theorists, especially Wertheimer (1912a, 1923), guided by their analysis of the experimental data, defined singularity as one of the pivotal concepts of the theory. It was built into many subsequent theories, including the present one. We have become quite adept at determining singularities experimentally, in specific cases. Unfortunately, here the analogy with the example from physics ends. There is still no theory to tell us how to predict singularities. The prospects for such a theory are dim, and probably depend on progress in neurophysiology. But the points to be made here are these: (1) We can establish the presence of singularities in particular instances by experiment, if not from a formula or general theory. (2) Regardless of how they are established, there is nothing vague about the role they play, e.g., in determining relative similarities. (3) No rival theory has a formula to determine "essential" or "psychologically effective" qualities within the stream of incoming stimulation. In fact, the main defect of rival theories is that they do not even recognize the need for differentiating between "essential" and "nonessential" or, as we say, singular and nonsingular stimulus properties.–E.G.]

whole qualities. We found that an essential factor in phenomenal relevance is the degree of singularity. Only insofar as the qualities are also singular, or to the extent to which they are singular, do they determine the phenomenal picture, and thus similarity. This is stated here in full generality, not restricted to distortions. The grouping as well—at least in the narrower sense of relatedness of parts—is determined by the tendency to result, as much as is compatible with the stimulus configuration, in *singular* whole qualities.

This tendency can be illustrated by, for instance, Experiments 27 and 28 of Chapter 4: clearly 27 can be considered as a "main experiment" and 28 as a "control experiment." Similar considerations apply to the "factor of proximity," which, to emphasize what is meant here, can be reformulated as "Everything else being equal, the smaller of two measurements is the more singular one."

3. *The phenomenal picture and the manner of comprehension.* Similarity is a relation not between stimulus complexes but between their phenomenal pictures. Now in some circumstances the same stimulus complex *may be comprehended* differently by different observers, and even by the same observer at different times. These differences, as they are differences in the phenomenal picture, should influence the judgment of similarity by decreasing unanimity among the Os. The resulting spread in the similarity judgments is, then, not only explained but even expected under the same conditions and in the same direction in which phenomenal ambiguity tends to occur.

Outright ambiguity is rare with our experimental material because we purposely gave preference to unambiguous designs in order to obtain clear-cut results. Even under these conditions, however, ambiguity often increased with the transition from a singular to a nonsingular quality. In Experiment 45, for instance, 45a may appear as "imperfectly symmetrical"; 45b is then "still less symmetrical," and 45c is "just about as imperfectly symmetrical as the St." For another observer, however, this *approximate* symmetry may not be phenomenally effective. That is, the linear patterns of the two sides are not phenomenally related to each other; phenomenally, the form of each linear pattern emerges by itself and may be the effective criterion. In that case, 45b will be the more similar version. Both modes of comprehension are possible; neither is compelling—as the approximately equal distribution of choices between the two variants shows. Quite similar ambiguities also occur in cases of nonsingular orientation in space, as will be demonstrated in Experiment 55 (see sections 43 and 47).

Differences in the *comprehension* of the figures are of course not the only reasons for differences in the choice of the more similar CF. Even when two figures are always comprehended in only one way the judgments of similarity may disagree considerably. This often happens when both CFs are about equally similar to the St, for instance in Experiment 43, where the choices are equally distributed between b and c. In this case there was never any indication that the figures might be comprehended in more than one way.

Although, for the reasons just mentioned, one might expect many judgments of "equal similarity," this rarely happened. Such judgments were intentionally discouraged by the wording of the instructions in the form of a leading question, "Which CF is the *more* similar?" This suggested to the subject that he choose, if at all possible, one of the two CFs. He was deliberately encouraged to make an effort to discover even the slightest difference in similarity. Otherewise many Os tend to make offhand judgments of—approximately—equal similarity.

This investigation was not concerned with discovering the basis of the ambiguity of many figures, nor with what determines, in an individual case, whether a figure is comprehended in one way or another. It was intended only to show that the reduction of similarity to the phenomenal pictures instead of to the stimulus complexes makes it possible to understand the occurrence of individual differences. Still, it does *not lead to* an assumption of *"arbitrary subjectivity"* as the basis of perceived similarity. For there are many cases in which, in general, only a single mode of comprehension is realized, or where even with an intentional attempt to change comprehension only a single version of structuring can be realized. And even in ambiguous cases not just any arbitrary structuring is possible; sometimes there are two possibilities, always only a finite number, and even then with different, usually predictably different, ease of realization.

6

THE ROLE OF SPATIAL ORIENTATION: INTERCHANGE OF WHOLE QUALITIES AND OF PART FUNCTIONS

40. THE PROBLEM: THE THEORIES OF MACH AND SACHS

There is a type of variation of figures for which it seemed that similarities could be directly explained by changes of a geometrical parameter without recourse to a mediating "change of the phenomenal picture." These are changes in similarity occasioned by rotation–tilting in the plane–and the similarity of two symmetrical figures, which is related to rotation.

That orientation in space is important for perception and also for similarity of visual images can be documented with everyday observations. Photographs are difficult to recognize upside down, and how difficult it is to recognize tilted objects becomes obvious after one look into a storage attic (see also Lewin, 1923, p. 210). While the distance of an object from the observer and its direction in relation to him are both largely irrelevant, [1] its orientation in space plays, phenomenally, a considerable role in perception. There is size constancy, and one might speak of directional constancy, but there is not, with the same degree of reliability, a "tilt constancy."

Laws about changes of similarity with rotation were proposed by Mach (1902, pp. 106–121) and Sachs (1897). We base this discussion mainly on the ideas of Sachs, which essentially coincide with Mach's. The differences between them will be taken up in section 42 below.

[1] An exception is the well-known moon illusion (see Schur, 1925). [Since this footnote was written in 1936, Rock and Kaufman (1962) have shown that this exception is only apparent and is reducible to an instance of size constancy.–E.G.]

Sachs assumes that optical perception depends to a large extent on eye motions. He deduces from the anatomy of the oculomotor system that the visual image depends especially on the *directions* of the eye movements, independent of the magnitude of the motion. This assumption then permits conclusions about similarity with changes of direction, including rotation. We will not discuss the physiological basis of this theory because it presupposes perception by means of movement of the muscles, an assumption which–since Stratton's experiments (1902)–can no longer be maintained. This discussion will be confined to the ideas about similarity which he deduced from it.

Sachs's conclusions were:

1. When one of two congruent figures is rotated–tilted in its plane–in relation to the other, the greater the angle of rotation, the less its similarity to the stationary figure. Dissimilarity is greatest with a 180° rotation (Sachs, 1897, p. 24).

2. Because the human oculomotor system is symmetrical with respect to the median plane, two figures which are related to each other as image and mirror image are particularly similar to each other if the plane of reflection coincides with the median plane (see also Mach, 1902, pp. 106 and 110). It seems that the possibility of mirror images reflected by a plane tilted against the median plane did not occur to Sachs (or Mach).

These two conclusions will be tested and the results compared with ideas developed here.

41. THE EXPERIMENTAL PROCEDURES

The procedures used here permitted the examination of both questions simultaneously with a small number of experiments. The tests were made with a single figure, symmetrical within itself. If a figure with one single axis of symmetry is rotated in its own plane it is always, i.e., with every angle of rotation, transformed into its mirror image in such a way that the plane of reflection bisects the angle of rotation and is perpendicular to the plane of rotation.

The following example will help to visualize this. Figure 49 shows a symmetrical figure in three phases of rotation 50° apart. The axis of symmetry of 49a is inclined by 50° against the vertical, that of 49c by 50° to the other side. 49a and 49c are mirror images. Their respective line of reflection is the vertical. But 49a

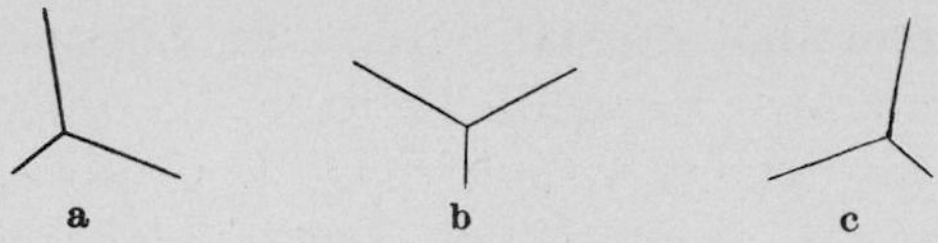

a b c

FIGURE 49

and 49b are also mirror images of each other. The line in which a is reflected to give b likewise bisects the angle of rotation, therefore it is inclined by 25° against the vertical. If one draws such a line to the left of 49a and constructs on it a mirror image to 49a, the result is a figure which lies a little above and to the left of the starting figure, the lines of which run parallel and in the same sense as those of 49b. 49b in our drawing is the mirror image of 49a, shifted by a parallel translation from the left of 49a to the right, and reflected on a straight line inclined by 25° against the vertical.[2]

The experimental procedure was as follows. A figure was presented through a 25 × 25 cm. opening in a large, fairly homogeneous field—a doorframe covered with paper. The aperture could be closed by means of a black cardboard shutter which slid up and down in a slot behind it. Behind this shutter was a wooden wheel which could be turned with click stops by steps of 5°, with the center of rotation at the center of the aperture. The drawings were attached to the wheel and were presented successively in various positions. The arrangement made it possible to create any number of mirror images of a St which differed from one another only in the inclination of the plane of reflection by which they were related to the St as mirror images. The shutter was closed during rotation so that the Os did not see the figures being rotated. The loud noise that accompanied the rotation was not recognizable as a rotation sound. In fact, quite a few Os did not notice until late in the course of the experiment that the same figure was being presented in different positions. When the Os became aware of this fact it did not appear to influence the results. The Os were asked, "Which of the two figures presented later appears more similar to the one presented first?" On re-

[2] The parallel translation makes recognition of these geometrical relationships difficult in our *illustration*. In the experiments it was of no consequence, since in the experiments with successive presentation all three figures were presented at the *same* place in space, and in the experiments with simultaneous presentation *both* CFs were shifted parallel to themselves against the St. The observability of the geometrical reflection corresponds, then, approximately to the situation in our illustration.

quest all three positions were presented again, in the same order, one or more times. The order of the CFs was alternated for different Os.

42. TEST OF THE THEORY OF MACH AND SACHS

Let us first consider the experiments from the point of view of reflection only.

In Experiment 49 the vertical plane of reflection is tested against a plane inclined by 25° against the vertical. CF 49c, which is reflected on the vertical, is the more similar for 10 of 10 Os.

In Experiment 50a, b, c, the vertical plane of reflection is tested against a plane inclined by 20°; in Experiment 51a, b, c, against a plane inclined by 30°. Here again the CF reflected on the vertical is more similar: 50a $\sim$ c $\nsim$ b for 6 of 6 Os, 51a $\sim$ c $\nsim$ b for 9 of 10 Os.

With Figures 50 and 51 the *horizontal* also was investigated as the plane of reflection. In Experiment 50d, e, f, a horizontal

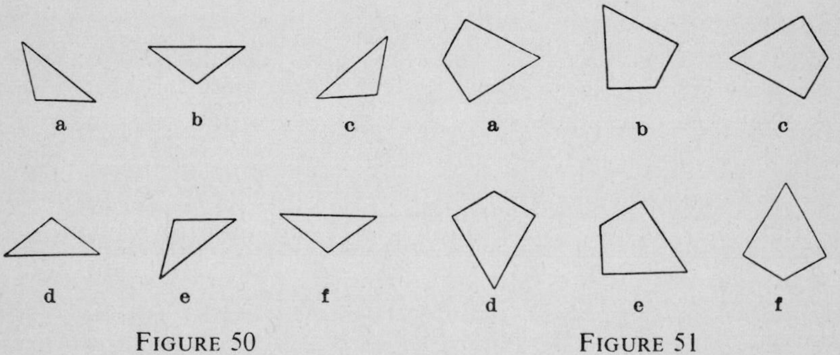

FIGURE 50 FIGURE 51

plane of reflection is tested against a plane inclined against the horizontal by 60°. In these experiments the CF reflected on the horizontal is the more similar: 50d $\sim$ f $\nsim$ e for 9 of 10 Os, 51d $\sim$ f $\nsim$ e for 10 of 10 Os.

Finally, in Experiment 52[3] one CF, 52b, is reflected on a plane inclined by 30° against the vertical, the other CF, 52c, on a

[3] This experiment, and also Experiments 59 and 60, could not be performed with the arrangement described in section 41, for reasons not related to these experiments. Instead, the figures were drawn on square sheets of white cardboard and presented simultaneously. The identity of the figures apart from their orientation was verified by means of transillumination with a strong light.

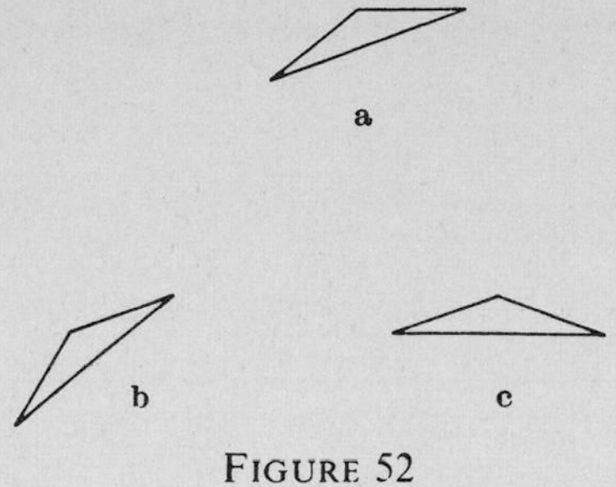

FIGURE 52

plane inclined by 10°. The former is more similar: 52a ∼ b ≁ c for 9 of 10 Os.

Images reflected on the vertical are, then, more similar (Experiments 49; 50a, b, c; 51a, b, c), as expected according to Sachs. Of the remaining cases, in Experiment 52 the variant reflected in a plane nearer to the vertical is not the more similar, and in Experiments 50d, e, f and 51d, e, f, the figure reflected on the horizontal (the worst possible case according to Sachs) is actually the most similar.

From the point of view of geometry, it is just as correct to consider the variations in Experiments 49, 50, 51, and 52 not as reflections but as *rotations in the plane.* When the plane of reflection is not the vertical this point of view is even more in the spirit of Sachs's theory, because he assumes that only reflections on the vertical conserve similarity. From that point of view, however, *all* the results disagree with Sachs's assumption, because in all cases the less similar CF is rotated either less than the more similar CF or, in Experiment 52, by the same amount.

According to Mach, too, reflection is similarity conserving only if the plane of reflection is the vertical. Experiment 50d, e, f, considered as a reflection experiment, is then to be counted against Mach. His theory, however, differs in one particular from Sachs's. Mach assumes that a 180° rotation produces a relatively similar figure. He reduces similarity to coincidence of directions, disregarding the sense of the direction. The minimum of similarity should, then, be expected with a 90° rotation (Mach himself did not elaborate on this point). This would explain the result of Experiment 50d, e, f—considered as a rotation experiment—because CF 50f, which is rotated through 180°, is the more similar. Experiment 52, however, must be counted against Mach.

Here both CFs are rotated through only 20°, but patently are not of equal similarity to the St. In addition, neither CF can be considered as a vertical mirror image. The Mach-Sachs theory similarly fails for almost all of the following experiments (see especially Experiments 60a, b, d; 61, and 62).

43. QUALITIES DEPENDENT ON POSITION: SYMMETRY

We now ask whether here, as in the cases dealt with before, it is possible to develop criteria for similarity based on the *phenomenal picture* of the figures. This amounts to asking whether there are phenomenal qualities of the whole or its parts which vary with orientation in space. The question here is not how one figure is derived from another, or how it might be thought of as being derived from another. Rather, each figure is considered with respect to its own phenomenal qualities. Are there qualities which are not equally realized in different spatial orientations?

The demonstration of dependence on spatial orientation is easiest in the case of *symmetry.* We begin with figures which have *several axes of symmetry.* The St in Experiment 53 is a square (53a and d). One CF is a rectangle (53b and e), the other a

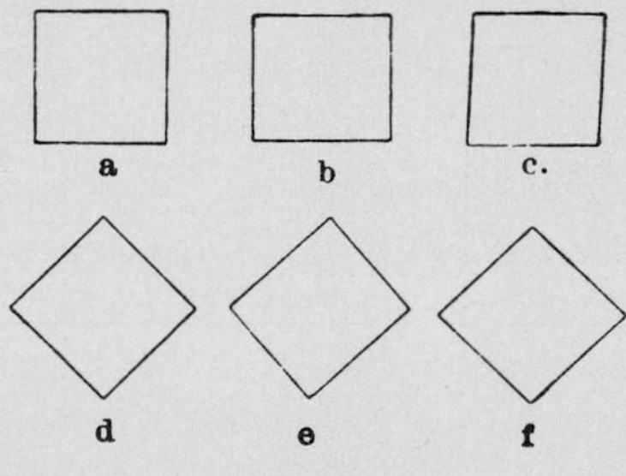

FIGURE 53

rhomboid (53c and f). Consider first Figure 53a, b, c. In 53b the symmetry about the diagonal axes is destroyed, in 53c that about the vertical and horizontal axes. We now make the assumption that geometrical symmetry is *preferentially realized* with a vertical orientation of the axis of symmetry; second in effectiveness is a horizontal orientation; and least effective are oblique axes. This agrees with the result of Experiment 53a, b, c: $a \sim b \nsim c$ for 10 of 10 Os. In a second experiment, 53d, e, f, the three figures are rotated; geometrically they are still the same figures, but now the *diagonals* of the square coincide with the vertical and the horizontal. According to our assumption, the rectangle, in which the symmetry about these axes is destroyed, should now be less similar. This expectation is confirmed: 53d $\sim$ f $\nsim$ e for 10 out of 10 Os.

In this pair of experiments, of two CFs *first one and then the other* is more similar to the St depending on the spatial orientation in which *all three figures* are presented. The phenomenal consequences of the rotations are that different qualities are realized in the St as well as in the CFs. The square is seen as symmetrical not in *all* its geometrical axes of symmetry but preferentially in those occupying the vertical and the horizontal. In 53a it appears as a special case of a rectangle, i.e., with singular right angles but a nonsingular ratio of the adjacent sides. [4] In 53d, on the other hand, it appears as a special case of a rhomboid, i.e., with singular equality of the adjacent sides but nonsingular angles. [5] This corresponds to differences in the internal relatedness of the lines to which Schumann (1900) called attention. In 53a opposite sides are phenomenally related, in d adjoining sides.

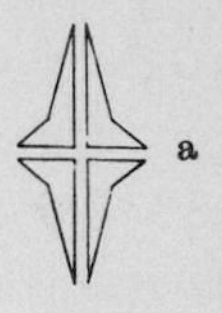

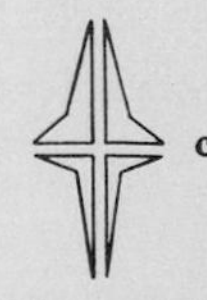

FIGURE 54

The following experiment examines, by the same method, the symmetry about a vertical axis against that about a horizontal axis. Figure 54a is symmetrical about both axes. In 54b and c two quadrants are changed in the same way; thus geometrically the change is of equal extent in both cases. In 54b the right half of the figure is changed, in 54c the lower half. Figure 54b, then, is symmetrical only about the horizontal axis, 54c only about the vertical. The experimental result was that 54c was more similar for 10 of 12 Os. When all three figures are rotated through 90°, the symmetry relationships are reversed, and so is the result for 9 of 12 Os.[6]

Finally, in Experiment 55 simple symmetry is tested against

[4] Schneider (1932) found that of all rectangles the square is least sensitive to change in the ratio of the sides. His figures were always oriented as in 53a and b.

[5] For a discussion of the nonsingularity of right angles in this orientation, see section 48.

[6] [This result has since been the subject of a detailed analysis by Rock and Leaman (1963).–E.G.]

changes in nonsingular qualities (see legend to Figure 55), somewhat as in Experiment 39. Aside from orientation, 55a = 55d, b = e, and c = f. In Experiment 55a, b, c the result is $a \sim c \nsim b$ for 9 of 10 Os; one O was unable to make a choice. When the figures were turned so that the short side became the base, as in 55d, e, f, the result was reversed: in 10 out of 10 cases $55d \sim e \nsim f$. It is then immediately apparent that 55d and e are symmetrical, whereas f is

FIGURE 55

Measurements (in mm. and cm.[2]) of the actual figures used:

	Base	Height above base	Right* side	Left side	Height above right** side	Height above left side	Area
d	70	85	92	92	64	64	29.5
e	71.5	76	84.5	84.5	65	65	27.5
f	66.5	89.5	92	99.5	64	60	29.6

* In 55a, b, c base.
** In 55a, b, c height above base.

asymmetrical (see Rubin, 1921, p. 131). This symmetry, however, is not realized with an oblique orientation of the axis of symmetry. Finally, when 55d, e, and f were rotated through 90° so that the axes of symmetry were horizontal, judgments became variable: of 12 Os, 5 chose the symmetrical CF, 55e, and 7 chose 55f. The 5 Os who chose 55e gave as their reason either the symmetry ("e is more a pyramid"), or the difference in the directions of the figures in space connected with the symmetry ("f goes too much downward"). For the 7 Os who chose f, the lower edge running up on a slant became the base. These Os then saw the figures about as in 55a, b, c. The appearance might be formulated as "a, b, c, somewhat slanted." Here, too, it is apparent that the same figure "looks different" depending on its orientation in space and specifically on its orientation with respect to the vertical and horizontal.

44. FOUR PROPOSITIONS TO EXPLAIN THE RESULTS

In the last experiments, even when all three figures were rotated, their orientation in space *relative to one another* was unchanged.[7] Thus Mach's and Sachs's ideas about the effect of rotation are not applicable since they refer only to *differences of mutual orientation.* Rather, the explanation here necessarily depends on changes in the phenomenal pictures due to differences of orientation in space. This suggests that the results presented in section 42 on rotated figures can also be interpreted in this way.

The results can be explained on the basis of the following phenomenological findings:

1. Two directions in space are singled out, the vertical and the horizontal. This statement hardly needs elaboration since it is well grounded experimentally (see, among many others, the experiments of Oppenheimer, 1934).

2. Among the functions of the parts of a figure are those which are determined to some degree by the orientation to the two distinguished axes, the vertical and the horizontal. Some of these functions are of such saliency that the language has words for a part of a figure in that particular function, e.g., "base."

The conditions which in general govern whether in a particular figure a function arises which depends on orientation will not be investigated here. Surely not every figure gives rise to, say, a base; for instance, a star-shaped figure will not. But even if there is a part which is horizontal and lowermost it need not be conceived as a typical "base"; in a regular decagon, for example, even when one side is horizontal, this side is coordinated with the remaining ones for reasons of figural structure, and therefore a base function will not be realized. On the other hand, a base-like function may develop even in the absence of a bottom horizontal: in Figure 49a and c, for example, where the two lower lines function as "legs" ("pedestal function"); similarly if 55d, e, f (turned sideways) are conceived as 55a, b, c "not quite properly oriented."

3. The two principal directions of space are not on an equal footing. The vertical separates phenomenally equivalent domains, the two "sides," whereas the horizontal separates phenomenally nonequivalent domains, "up" and "down." This is well illustrated by the fact that even adults easily mistake right and left, while even children can tell up from down.

[7] Aside from slight changes in 55a, b, c and still slighter changes in Experiment 53.

4. Many figures have, as wholes, *preferred,* distinguished, or singular *positions.* This fact is most noticeable in figures which have one long extension. Such figures "stand" or "lie," and phenomenally they stand "straight" or are "tilted." For these impressions it is not always necessary nor even possible that any part of the figure have the orientation which belongs phenomenally to the entire figure. In the case of a "standing" ellipse only a very small piece of the periphery is actually vertical; truly vertical is only the long axis, which is not necessarily drawn in. The design in Figure 56 is "standing straight," even though no single piece of the outline is vertical. Here again, it is the fact that this

FIGURE 56

phenomenon exists that is of interest, not the conditions which bring it about.

45. EXPLANATION OF EXPERIMENTS 49; 50a, b, c; 51a, b, c

It now remains to discover how far the other experiments described in this chapter can be understood from this point of view. This is most easily demonstrated on figures reflected on the vertical axis.

To discuss first the functions of parts: in both 49a and c the two lower lines are functionally "pedestals" or "legs" of the upper oblique line. The exchanged positions of the short and long "legs" is phenomenally of little consequence because right and left are phenomenally equivalent according to assumption 3 of section 44. Likewise, the direction of the upper oblique line does not have individual value since in both instances it is nonsingular. Geometrical symmetry is not realized in either figure. CF 49b, on the other hand, has an entirely different structure. Here the two long rays are coordinated. The geometrical axis of symmetry coincides with the singular vertical and is realized as the axis of symmetry.

As for the character of the whole, 49a and c are "broad-based, resting," whereas b is "standing on one leg," "reaching up."

All three figures in Experiment 49 are "upright." They are so oriented that singular extensions coincide with singular spatial directions: in a and c the (undrawn) line connecting the lower ends of the two "legs," in b the axis of symmetry. For this reason the structuring as described is compelling. If 49a were so oriented that the two lower lines were not unequivocally "down," a structuring as in 49b, or in still other ways, might result in addition or even preferentially. The cogency of the structuring and the unanimity of the results are largely consequences of this circumstance (see section 50 for a more detailed discussion of this point).

Similar considerations apply to Experiments 50a, b, c and 51a, b, c. In these experiments too, the less similar CF lacks the conditions for a structuring like that of the St. A different, but stable, structuring is suggested by the fact that in both cases a side which was oblique in the St falls into the horizontal and thus becomes endowed with the singular function of a "base." Specifically, 50a and c have a lower base and two "oblique, asymmetrical sides." CF 50b has a "terminal line" at the top and two oblique, dependent, symmetrical sides. Over-all, 50a and c are standing figures with oblique extensions. They "*stand* upright, but *are* slanting." CF 50b does not stand, it hangs. It "*hangs* straight" and "*is* straight." Likewise, 51a and c have equal functions of the parts, phenomenally a horizontal axis and no bases, whereas in 51b the short side functions as a base. In a and c the adjoining long sides are homologous by symmetry, and so are the short sides. In 51b it is rather that opposite sides belong together, as "base and lid" and as "sides" of a distorted trapezoid with the long side up. Over-all, 51a and c are "stretched," "pointed," and horizontal; 51b is "massive," "blunt," and vertical.

46. INTERPRETATION OF EXPERIMENTS 50d, e, f AND 51d, e, f

Experiments 50d, e, f and 51d, e, f can be understood in the same way. In 50d and f the long side coincides with the singular horizontal and is the main line of the figure; in 50e one of the short sides is so singled out. In 50d and f the short sides are coordinated as "partners," in 50e all three sides have different functions. Phenomenally, 50d and f are symmetrical, and 50e is asymmetrical. CF 50f has the same structure as the St, differing from it only in orientation; 50e is an "entirely different triangle." According to the reports of the Os, the rotation which changes the St into 50f is realized; the smaller rotation leading to 50e is not.

Even without actual experiments it is easy to demonstrate that under suitable conditions a 180° rotation is realized as a rotation. For instance, a 9 is easily seen as an inverted 6. But this realization occurs only if the structuring is the same in both orientations. For instance, a 2 is not spontaneously seen as an inverted figure 7 the lower part of which ends in a 6: Ꞁ.

The changes brought about by rotation in Figure 51d, e, f must be considered somewhat differently. Frequently 51f appears not as an inversion of the St, but as the St *distorted* in a nonsingular parameter. That is, the long lines and the short lines have *"exchanged" their identities.* In this distortion the lateral corners seem merely shifted downward. But, as in the previous cases, the structuring is the same as that of the St, whereas in the dissimilar CF, 51e, the structuring differs. This is again shown most clearly by the relationships between the parts. In 51d and f the two short sides and the two long sides belong together by symmetry. In 51e one long side is the base, and the other three sides are an "irregular upper boundary."

47. DEPENDENCE OF SYMMETRY ON ORIENTATION

The salience of symmetry with a vertical orientation of the axis follows from assumption 3, section 44, since in this orientation symmetrical parts are coordinated by their direction in space as well. Whether symmetry will also be dominant in determining structure in other positions depends on what other potentially "good" structurings are inherently possible in the figure. In Experiment 39, for instance, the symmetrical CF appears more similar to the St (9 of 10 Os) even when orientation of the figures is horizontal. This figure is so long and narrow that in any position the parts which are homlogous by symmetry will belong together because of their proximity. From this point of view, the triangles of Figure 55 are much more open to different structurings. Here one *side* can be singled out by virtue of its horizontal position (55a, b, c). But even if the axis of symmetry falls into the distinctive horizontal, as in d, e, f rotated 90°, the correlation of the symmetrical halves is not *inescapable.* Moreover, in this position another criterion, the differences in the length of the axis, and with it the length of the entire figure, emerge as relevant for similarity. In the horizontal position, 55d and f are of nearly the same length, while 55 e is considerably shorter. Even though this criterion depends on the axis being distinguished by its horizontal position, it does not depend on symmetry as such, which, in the horizontal, is less compelling. In this quality 55d and f agree more than do 55d and e.

48. POSITION DEPENDENCE OF THE SINGULARITY OF THE RIGHT ANGLE

In the following experiments, as in the preceding ones, geometrically symmetrical figures were used, but the differences in similarity in different positions are not due to either lack of or preservation of phenomenal symmetry. The St was a right angle with sides of equal length; the CFs were angles of 87°, 90°, and 93° with *sides three times as long.* Figures 57 and 58 show the four figures, once "hanging" and once "standing." In each of the two experiments, all three comparison figures were presented to 10 Os. After the most similar CF was chosen it was removed,

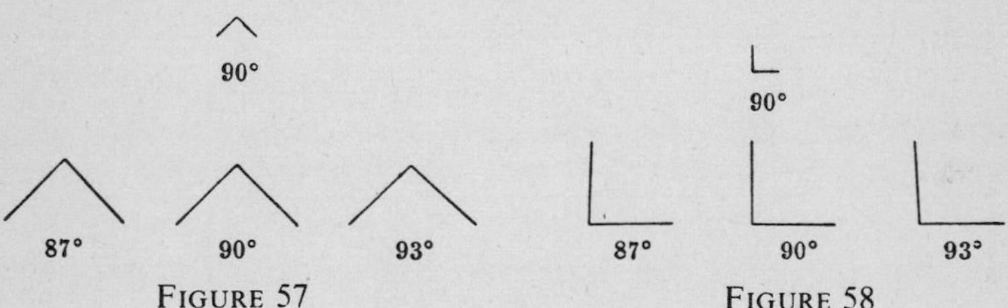

FIGURE 57 FIGURE 58

and the O was asked to choose the more similar of the remaining two CFs. Table 3 shows the results of these experiments.

TABLE 3
10 Os each in Experiment ∟ and in Experiment ∧

	∟			∧		
Number of Os choosing	93°	90°	87°	93°	90°	87°
in 1st place	0	10	0	4	3	3
in 2nd place	4/2*	0	4/2+6*	3	5	2

*In this experiment 6 of the 10 Os chose CF 87° in second place, and 4 considered CFs 93° and 87° to be equally similar.

When the angles were "standing," the *rectangular* CF was the most similar for all 10 Os. When the angles were "hanging," the 90° angle no longer stood out and the distinction of the CF with the same angle as the St vanished; the three CFs are equally similar to it. The result might also be expressed as follows: the sensitivity to change of a right angle with sides of equal length is considerably greater if it is "standing" than if it is "hanging." This, too, is explainable according to our assumptions. When a right angle is standing, both sides fall on singular directions. A change of the angle in the CF destroys this coincidence between the sides of the angle and singular directions. The sides of a hanging right angle, on the other hand, are not anchored to a preferred spatial direction, and a change in the size of the angle does not disrupt such an anchoring.

49. ROTATION OF NONSYMMETRICAL FIGURES

These explanatory principles are not restricted to symmetrical figures. The only reason for using them here is that it is particularly easy to invent symmetrical figures which in certain positions achieve a stable structure without phenomenal symmetry. Figure 59 shows a nonsymmetrical variant of Figure 49: all three rays of Figure 59 are angled in the middle in the same direction.[8] Here

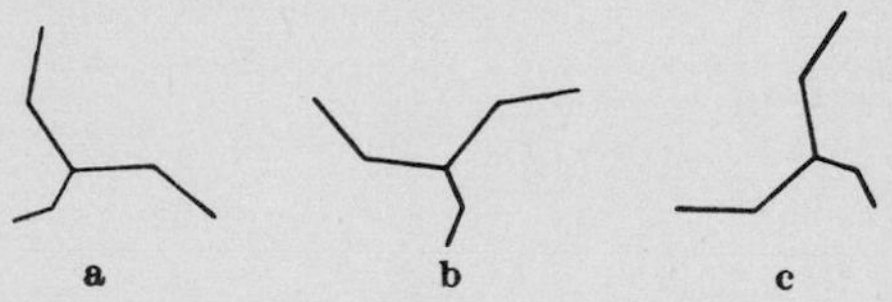

a b c

FIGURE 59

also a $\sim$ c $\nsim$ b (15 of 20 Os). The analysis of the differences in the structure of the figures is also the same (see section 42). But here the result is not as clear-cut, mainly because CF 59b has, phenomenally, a less stable position than 49b. Because of its lack of symmetry, 59b *has no axis* which could assume a singular position. The figure appears to be "not quite properly oriented," as some of the Os put it. For this reason it sometimes appeared as the St in a rotated position, which did not happen with Figure

[8] For the experimental arrangements, see footnote 3 above.

49b where the orientation is a singular one. Nevertheless, the judgment $a \sim c \nsim b$ is plainly in the majority, even though 59b is rotated less than 59c, and even though c is not even phenomenally the mirror image of a.

50. SINGULARITY OF POSITION

To confirm these ideas, Experiment 60 was performed.[9] This figure is an asymmetrical version of Figure 50. CF 60b is rotated

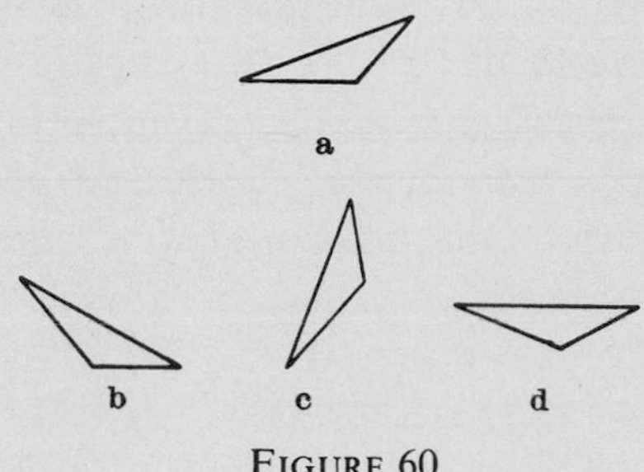

FIGURE 60

so that the shorter of the two oblique sides of the St, 60a, coincides with the horizontal, making it phenomenally the base. The former base takes over the function of the shorter oblique side; the long oblique retains its function. Rotation results in an exchange of functions, but all the functions of the St are found in the CF, even though some have been taken over by new carriers. Thus the two figures have the same organization and structure without being mirror images of one another.

This CF was first offered along with 60c. Geometrically 60c is also identical with the St, and is rotated by the same amount as 60b, only in the opposite sense. According to Sachs's theory, the two CFs should be equally similar to the St. This was in fact the result: of 18 Os, 10 chose 60b and 8 chose 60c. But this choice is not uniquely determined by our principles either, because CF 60c does not derive a unique structure from its orientation. As it is positioned, none of the sides falls on a singular direction. The figure as a whole is *phenomenally oblique.* However, the nearest stable position is that of the St. For this reason there is a tendency to see the figure as "rotated out of that position." This tendency

[9] For the experimental arrangements, see footnote 3 above.

is so strong that in some Os, especially naïve ones and children, it even intrudes into the motor system: O turns his head or inadvertently takes the sheet and turns it so the the figure comes into the position of the St. The striking feature of this reaction is that such a tendency *never occurs for the other CF which is rotated by the same amount.* Phenomenally, then, the choice here is between a CF (60c) which has the "wrong" orientation but is identical with the St, and a "correctly" oriented CF (60b) which, however, differs from the St in having right and left exchanged and in being somewhat distorted.

In a second experiment, CF 60b was presented with 60d. CF 60d is rotated in the same sense as 60b but only far enough to bring the long side into the horizontal—that is, it is rotated *less* than 60b. In this position, however, the structure of the figure is changed from that of the St in a much more stable manner. The long side, which now tends to become the "base" because of its length alone, is also distinguished by its orientation. Although the absolute amount of rotation is larger in 60b than in 60d, the result is 60a $\sim$ b $\nsim$ d for 9 of 10 Os, this time *against Sachs's hypothesis.*

51. TENDENCY OF NONSINGULAR ORIENTATIONS TOWARD SINGULAR ONES: RESULTS

Here, then, it is not the changed direction of the various parts to the eye which compels a change in the impression of the figure, *but the change of the phenomenal structure produced by the altered orientation with respect to the main spatial axes,* that is, the change in functions and distribution of weights of the natural parts, and of certain whole qualities such as symmetry, standing, lying, hanging, and others. Every figure tends toward singular orientations. When it is presented in a singular, stable orientation, it structures itself accordingly. When it is presented in a nonsingular orientation, it is structured according to the nearest possible singular orientation and it appears as turned out of this position. In such cases the impression may be quite labile, if there are several neighboring singular orientations, with different resulting organizations, competing with each other.

In Figure 61, CF b appears as slightly "tilted." There is a tendency to put the bottom side (1, Figure 61b) into the horizontal.

Even though 61b is geometrically identical with 61a, it appears distorted. Geometrically it is not side 1 but side 2 (Figure 61b) that corresponds to the base of 61a. Consequently Figure 61c, *which is not geometrically identical* with the St but appears less distorted, seems more similar than 61b to 10 out of 10 Os. Next,

FIGURE 61

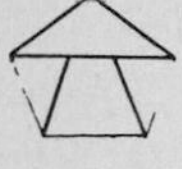

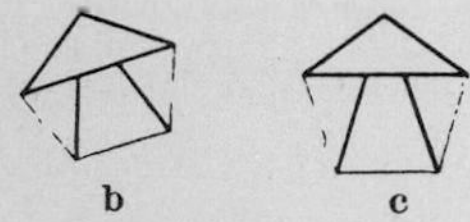

FIGURE 62

In the actual figures used, the three fainter lines were green.

61b is turned 90° so that side 2, which is geometrically homologous to the base of the St, becomes lowermost, without, however, becoming entirely horizontal. The figure is then oriented as shown in Figure 62b (disregarding the interior lines). Now rotation into the nearest singular position would result in a figure which agrees completely with the St; and now Figure 61b seems, to 4 of 10 Os, more similar than 61c. Next (Figure 62), interior lines are added which make the homology more compelling. The similarity of the geometrically identical but rotated CF is now still more pronounced: 62a $\sim$ b $\nsim$ c for 7 of 10 Os. But even now 3 Os prefer a slightly distorted CF to the rotated one.

Thus geometrical rotation may have several different *phenomenal* consequences: change in structuring as in 51b, distortion as in 51f, phenomenal rotation as in 50f and 62b, and finally combinations of these, as in 61b rotation + distortion, and mixed cases in which several possible impressions are in competition, as in 60c. At what degree of rotation the various changes of the phenomenal picture occur depends entirely on the structure of the particular figure. This is why the geometrical angle of rotation does not furnish a meaningful measure of the change of similarity. Rotations, too, obey the rule (see section 34) that phenomenal changes are not proportional to the degree of geometrical change, in this case rotation, but change by jumps. Angles of rotation, too, have sharply defined singular values along with vaguely defined ranges of nonsingular values.

52. RECTANGULARITY OF THE FRAME OF REFERENCE

Up to now we have called the singular directions in space simply the horizontal and the vertical. This is not intended to refer to the physical directions as determined by gravity. In fact, most of the experiments were made with the drawings lying horizontal on a table. In this situation the rectangular borders of the sheets take on the function of the singular directions. The results are also invariant to small rotations of the entire sheets. *The frame of reference remains the nearest directly enclosing system.* Even the orientation in relation to the median of the body or head is not necessarily decisive. It was therefore of interest to determine if at least *rectangularity* of the two singular axes was always required.

In Experiment 11 it was found that the right side of 11a was phenomenally homologous to the left side of 11c (see section 10). If Figure 11 were standing "straight," if its outside lines were vertical, this homology could be deduced from point 3 in section 44. As it happens, however, the regions to the right and to the left of the "axis" are not equivalent when the axis is not exactly perpendicular to the "base."

Similar considerations apply to the following pair of experiments. In Experiment 63 a small triangle is contained in a frame consisting of a rectangle and a large triangle. The little triangle is

FIGURE 63 FIGURE 64

varied in exactly the same way as is the middle line in Experiment 11. The small triangles in 63a and c are not isosceles but are mirror images of one another: their tips are situated to the side of the mid-line. In 63b the triangle is equilateral; its tip is in the mid-line. The experimental result is 63a $\sim$ c $\nsim$ b for 9 of 10 Os, as might be expected on the basis of the symmetry relations.

In the next experiment the "frame" is tilted in an oblique direction in such a way that its new "axis" falls midway between the tips of the little triangles in 63a and b. Into this frame were inserted the same three little triangles as in Experiment 63. While the small triangles in 64a and c are still mirror images in relation to the objective (in this case edge-of-the-paper) vertical, 64a and b are, at least nearly, mirror images in relation to the mid-line of the frame. Now the result is 64a $\sim$ b $\nsim$ c for 10 of 10 Os.

In these experiments, then, the functionally equivalent regions are separated not by a line perpendicular to the base but by a line somewhat inclined from the vertical. Furthermore, the position and direction of this imaginary line are determined by the structure of the figure itself, by the organization and articulation of the field (see also Kopfermann, 1930, p. 352).

How far the effect of the field structure goes, and to what extent the static sense or the position of the median of the head determines the singularity of directions, cannot be decided here.[10] But the fact that the influence of the field structure may even disturb the rectangularity of the frame makes it unlikely that the entire explanation for the similarity of mirror images lies in the vertical symmetry of our visual system.

[10] [Much has been learned in this field since this was written. See particularly Rock (1966, Chapter 2).–E.G.]

7

SINGULARITIES IN SIMILARITY SPACE

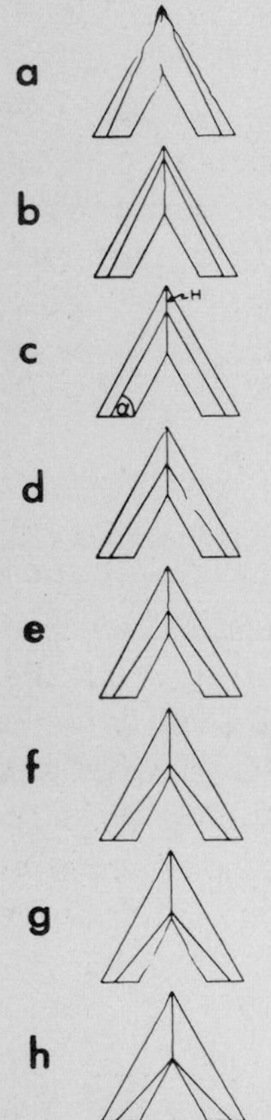

FIGURE 65

53. SERIAL VARIATION OF A PARAMETER ACROSS SINGULARITIES

The experiments to be presented in this chapter deal with a question only briefly discussed in section 38: What happens phenomenally when a geometric characteristic varies up to a singular value and then beyond it?

Consider the family of designs in Figure 65. The designs are identical in all but one aspect so that they form what, mathematically, is called a one-parameter family. The parameter which varies from design a to h is the angle α of the middle pair of lines against the base, or the height of the middle pair of lines from some reference point, say the apex of the outer lines, as indicated in Figure 65c. Either the height H or the angle α can be used to characterize each member of the family, although equal increments of one do not correspond to equal increments of the other. An infinite number of other characteristics could have been designated as the parameter being varied. Figure 66A shows the heights, so defined, marked off on a line. The origin, O, corresponds to the height of the apex of the outer lines, which is also the highest possible point for the middle lines. Figure 66B shows the same designs marked off, using the value of the angle α to fix the position of each design on the line. The order of the

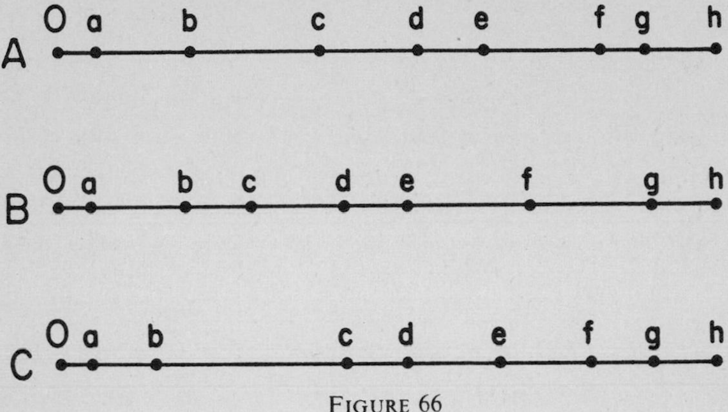

FIGURE 66

designs is the same on both lines, but the relative distances, the *scales* along the lines, are different. The degree of variation is thus not uniquely specified. "How much" variation there is from 65b to 65c or from 65f to 65g depends on which mathematical characteristic is chosen as the parameter. Each choice results in a particular relation of distances along the line representing this family of designs.

54. THE RANKING PROCEDURE: EXPERIMENT 65

Corresponding to the relations of difference among the designs of Figure 65, there are degrees of phenomenal dissimilarity among them. In the following experiment this series of designs [1] was presented to 15 Os, c as the St and the other seven designs as CFs. The Os were instructed to select the one CF most similar to the St. After the choice was made, the CF chosen was removed and the Os had to select the most similar CF from among those remaining. This procedure was repeated until the last possible choice had been made. The experiment resulted in a rank order, starting from c, of

[1] The designs in Figures 65, 70, 72, and 79 were available on printed sheets prepared for another experiment. They were cut out and pasted on individual white 3 × 5″ cards. The St was placed on a table before the O, then all the CFs were presented in random order below the St.

Designs 67, 69, 73, and 75 were larger, drawn with a black-ink felt pen on white 5 × 8″ cards, and presented in the same manner.

	d	e	b	f	a	g	h
c	1.3	2.3	2.7	4.5	4.8	5.7	6.9

But this tabulation fails to convey the obvious fact that a and b lie on one side of c, and d, e, f, g, and h on the other. To indicate both the degree of similarity and the direction in which the differences are presumed to lie, the rankings are rewritten as

			b		a		
c	1.3	(2.3	2.7)	(4.5	[4.8)	5.7]	6.9
	d	e		f		g	h

Disregarding brackets and parentheses, and reading the top row from right to left, then c, then the bottom row from left to right, the sequence is a, b, c, d, e, f, g, h. This tabulation also shows that d and e are closer to c than is b; that a is farther from c than are b, d, e, and f; and that g and h, in that order, are still farther. The numbers are the mean rankings. Those which were *not* significantly different ($p > .05$) by Tukey's multiple-range test are bracketed together, in sometimes overlapping brackets and parentheses. This procedure was followed for all rankings in this chapter. Tukey's multiple-range test was applied to all rankings, chi square to all individual comparisons.[2] Figure 66C is drawn to these specifications. The same experiment was carried out with f as the St, using another 15 Os. The resulting rank order was

		e		d	c	b	a
f	(1.2	2.1)	(3.5	3.8)	(5.0	[5.9)	6.6]
	g		h				

Reading again from a to f to h, the order is preserved. The order and the brackets and parentheses indicate that e is less similar to f than is g but significantly more similar than is h, and that d, c, b, and a are increasingly dissimilar to f, more so than is h. The brackets and parentheses tell us that c, b, and b, a, are not significantly different in rank, but that c and a differ significantly. This furnishes additional constraints on the representation of

[2] In these 1 × 2 matrices with 1 d.f., chi square was calculated without Yates's correction, as suggested by Katti (1968).

similarities as distances on line 66C. As it is drawn, Figure 66C is of the same length from O to h as are 66A and 66B. The remaining points are marked in such a way as to reflect the rank orders resulting from the two experiments: e.g., c-a $>$ c-f, etc. The points are not uniquely determined but are quite tightly constrained by the two rankings. Negatively, these experiments demonstrate that similarity does not vary parallel with either one of the two simple and obvious geometric parameters. Positively, they show that phenomenally c and d are closer together and more "central" than either of the two parametrizations indicate. The pattern was designed so that only in c are the middle lines parallel to the inner and outer lines; while in d, and also e, they are more centered, equidistant, balanced, or neutral. Since they were pivoted about their lower ends, which are nearer to the outer lines than to the inner ones, they could not simultaneously achieve parallelity and a position midway between the inner and outer lines. Consequently, instead of a sharp peak of singularity at which the phenomenal picture differs sharply from the neighboring patterns, there is a broader region of singularity, centered on c and d, with e on the right nearer to it than b on the left. Both c and d are somewhat singular members of this family, relatively isolated from a and b on the one hand and from e, f, g, and h on the other.

The difference between the three groups of designs is caused by the factor of proximity (Wertheimer, 1923). In 65a and b the middle lines are nearer to the outer lines; in f, g, and h they are nearer to the inner lines; in c and d, and also e, they are more on an equal footing with the inner and outer lines. As the parameter ranges from a to h the three regions are traversed in succession. Hypothesis I applies.

55. RANK-ORDER INVERSION: EXPERIMENT 67

There would be an inversion in the sequence of a, b, then c, d, e, and then f, g, h if the two "unbalanced" clusters—a, b, and f, g, h—were more similar to each other than to the balanced cluster in between. Or, given the degree of similarity between inner and outer clusters, such an inversion would occur if the middle cluster were more balanced, or "better," than c, d, e actually are, and thus less similar to the other two. It would also come about if the inner and outer clusters were more similar to each other, that is, if the phenomenal difference between "inside" and "outside" were reduced. Both of these features are present in Figure 67.

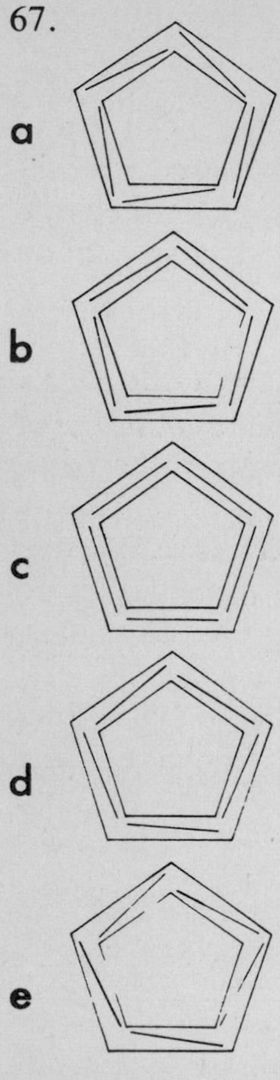

FIGURE 67

Inner and outer lines are more nearly of the same length; and the centers of the middle lines are equidistant from the inner and outer lines in all the variants, instead of being anchored at one end near the outer lines. Starting with 67a, designs b, c, d, and e are generated by turning the middle lines about their centers by successive small amounts. In a, b, d, and e the 10 ends of the five middle lines are near or far from the outer lines in an irregular way; in c the ends are exactly equidistant, making outer, middle, and inner lines all parallel. The figures are not symmetrical in themselves (although nearly so), nor are any of them mirror images because, as the design changes from a to e, two of the lines turn progressively in one sense and three in the opposite sense.

With a as the St, the rank order is (for 15 Os)

a	1.4	(2.3	2.5)	3.7
	b	e	**d**	**c**

The inversion e-d is not significant, but the inversion of c against d and e is significant ($p < .01$). (Significant inversions are indicated by the use of boldface type.) Even though the middle lines are turned less in c than in d and e, d and e are more similar to a than is c. Phenomenally it is not the degree of turning but the geometric divergence of the middle lines from the inner and outer lines which determines similarity. Zero divergence produces the singular phenomenal effect of "parallelity," which sets c apart from the variants with nonzero divergence. This being so, with c as the St similarity should decrease with increasing divergence, irrespective of the direction of the diverging lines. The experiment shows (for 15 Os)

b a
c (1.5 1.7) (3.3 3.5)
d e

There is no significant difference between the ranking of d and b, nor between e and a, which differ only in the *direction* of divergence, but there is a significant difference ($p < .01$) between d, b, on the one hand, both of which diverge less, and e, a, on the other hand, both of which diverge more.

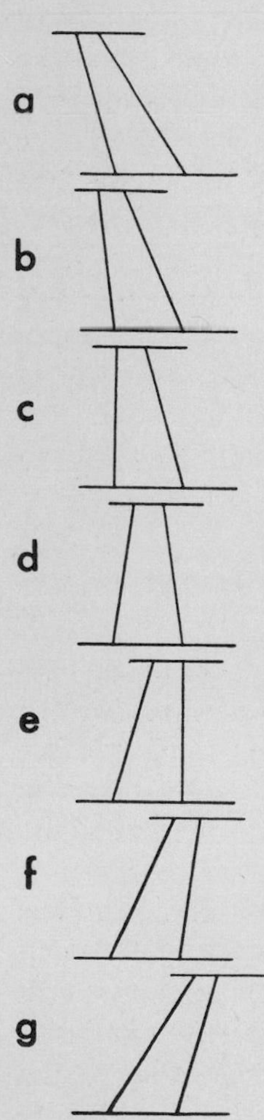

Figure 68

56. OTHER INSTANCES OF INVERTED RANK ORDER

In order to elucidate further this reversal of the rank order at singular values of the parameter, examples of different types of singularity and different kinds of parameter were tested.

In Figure 68, the slant of the vertical lines changes in steps of 8°. Except for the horizontals, b and f are mirror images of each other.

The figures were drawn in heavy black lines on 5 × 8″ white cards and presented in the same way as the designs in Experiment 65. With b as the St, the mean rankings for 15 Os are

a
b (1.7 1.8) (3.6 [4.3 4.5) 5.1]
c d f e g

The inversion f-e was not significant. However, when b was compared in a separate experiment with only f and e as CFs, $b \sim f \nsim e$ for 12 of 15 Os ($p < .05$). This result suggests that symmetry, and even near symmetry, can preserve similarity better than a smaller amount of unsymmetrical variation. This effect of symmetry was the first, and apparently the only, type of reversal to be observed previously. It was noted by Attneave (1950, p. 525), who remarked that "it actually introduces a new dimension" not anticipated in designing his experiment. The experiment also shows that individual judgments of similarity become less reliable when multiple choice–more than two CFs–is required, as it is in ranking several CFs in the experiments of this chapter. Therefore the rankings were supplemented in a few dubious instances, as here, by separate comparisons of only two CFs.

The next design, Figure 69, consists of eight dots. Four of these remain stationary, the other four are moved outward by increasing amounts (a to g). Figure 69a is pointed and concave; these qualities decrease in b and then reverse in c; d has neither points nor concavity–it is completely circular, and at the same time the design has increased in size.

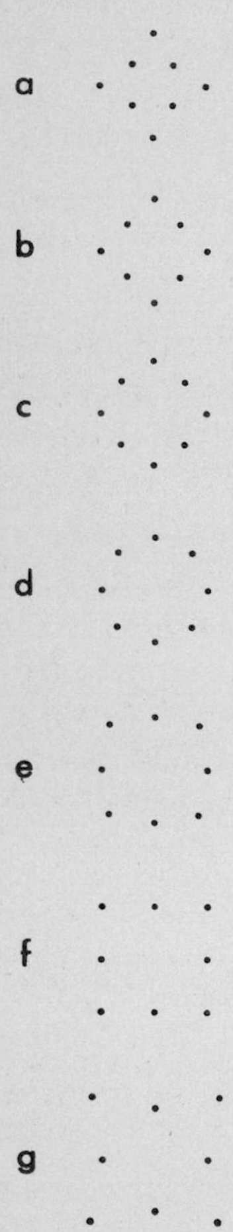

Beyond d it becomes pointed again and finally, at g, concave again. With g as the St, there is an inversion between a and d (for 10 Os):

	f	e	b	**a**	c	**d**
g	(1.2	[2.6)	(3.8	3.8	4.2]	5.4)

Design d is less similar than a, b, and c, but this difference is not quite significant. Therefore a further experiment tested g as the St against only a and d. The result was $g \sim a \nsim d$ for 14 of 15 Os ($p < .001$).

On the other hand, with the singular design d as the St the rank order faithfully follows the change in parameter (10 Os):

	c		b		a	
d	1.2	(2.2	2.6)	(4.5	[4.9)	5.6]
		e		f		g

The singular quality which leads to the disagreement between the geometric and the phenomenal sequences is circularity, as opposed to concavity and "having points." Other features, which have not been brought out, also play a part, particularly over-all size and relation to vertical and horizontal.

a b c d e f g

FIGURE 69

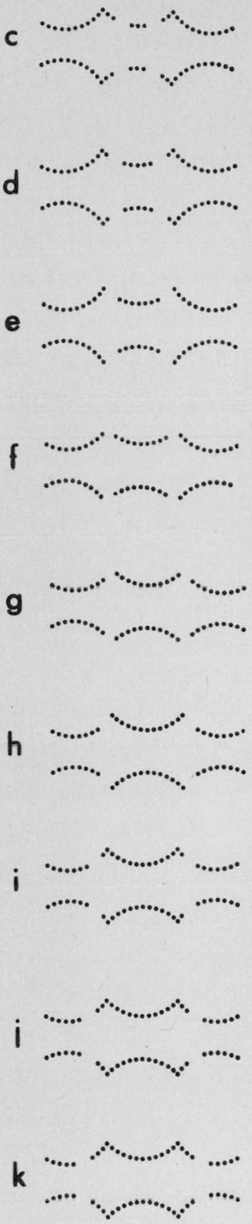

57. PROSTRUCTURAL VERSUS DISRUPTIVE GAPS: EXPERIMENT 70

The next three experiments form a group in which the variation consists in shifting four gaps along the lines of the design. Figure 70 shows the designs of the first of these experiments. They consist of dotted lines, with two dots missing in four symmetrical positions of the doubly symmetrical figure, creating four symmetrical gaps. The gaps are closest to the center in c, move outward in d, reach the corners in e, f, g, and h, and go on to the side curves in i, j, and k. Three experiments, each using 10 Os, were carried out, with d, f, and i as the Sts. The same ranking procedure was used as before.

```
             e                     d             c
f   (1.3  [3.4   {3.5)  (3.8  <5.7]  5.9}   6.1)  6.3>
      g            i      h           j            k
```

As before, the various parentheses and brackets combine those rankings which do *not* differ significantly ($p < .05$). The experiment suggests, or at least is compatible with, the representation presented in Figure 71A, where h and i are shown in their parametric order since the inversion in rank was far from significant.[3]

The same situation results with i as the St:

```
                  h       g        f    d    e      c
i   (1.4  [2.4  {3.1)  <3.4} ]  (5.5  5.7  6.3 >  6.6)
      j     k
```

FIGURE 70

Figure 71A therefore represents this experiment too fairly well, except for some change in

[3] With rank orders it is possible for a CF_1 to be *more* similar than a CF_2 and still rank *behind* CF_2 in average rank. E.g., if CF_1 is ranked first by 15 Os and fifth by 5 Os, its average rank is 2. If at the same time CF_2 is ranked second by those same 15 Os and first by the other 5 Os, its rank is 1.75. Thus CF_2 ranks ahead of CF_1, but $St \sim CF_1 \nsim CF_2$ for 15 of 20 Os ($p < .05$).

In the present instance the differences in rank and in similarity are in the same direction, even though not significantly so. But the possibility that the rank order might differ from the order of similarity should be kept in mind (see also footnote 4).

the relative distances and disregarding for the present the inverted order of d and e.

Finally, with d as the St, the result is

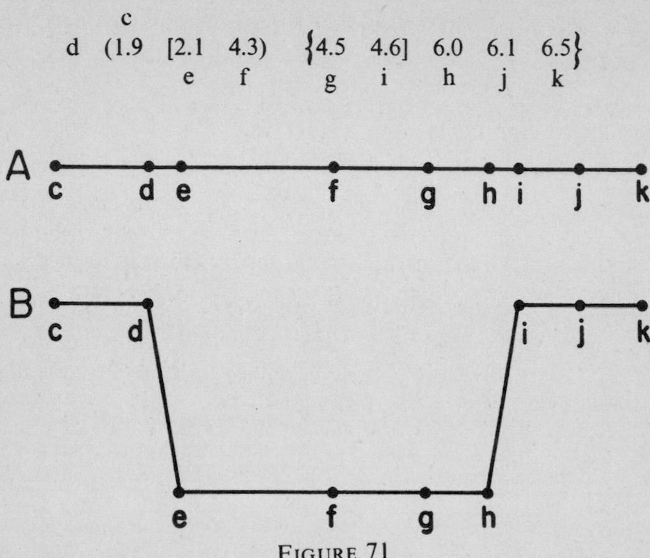

FIGURE 71

In this experiment there is an inversion in the order of h and i. While it falls short of significance both in the ranking and in individual choices (i was ranked before h by 7 of 10 Os, $p < .3$), it is in line with later results (section 58). Its consequences will therefore be considered.

The inversion in the sequence of h-i, as well as the earlier one, d-e—but not i-h with f as the St—can be represented in one diagram, 71B, but this diagram is not one-dimensional; instead, there is a two-dimensional array of points. As before, progression from left to right corresponds to the change of the parameter, i.e., shift of the gaps away from the center. But there is an additional phenomenal change, in another dimension, which occurs when the gap involves the corners, in Figure 70e, f, g, and h. The inversions, even though not significant, at least suggest that a gap within a line can be more similar to a gap within another line than to a gap at the end of a line or between two lines. The situation is comparable to the difference between Figures 29c and 29b. A gap *within* a line has the effect of interrupting something which, by the factor of good continuation (Wertheimer), forms one unit extending up to the corner. A gap *at the corner* separates two curves, just as does the corner itself when the curves are undisrupted. In this sense a gap at the corner is "prostructural," enhancing a subdivision already present; within the line it is "contrastructural."

58. STRONGER GAP EFFECTS: EXPERIMENTS 72, 73

A gap in a row of dots is not as compelling as a gap in a continuous line. In order to bring out the effect more clearly, another design was tested, using the line drawings shown in Figure 72 instead of the less well-defined dot patterns. The variation consisted in shifting the gaps toward the center line in steps of one gap width. Three experiments were performed, each using 10 Os. Again rankings bracketed together are not significantly different from each other. The results were:

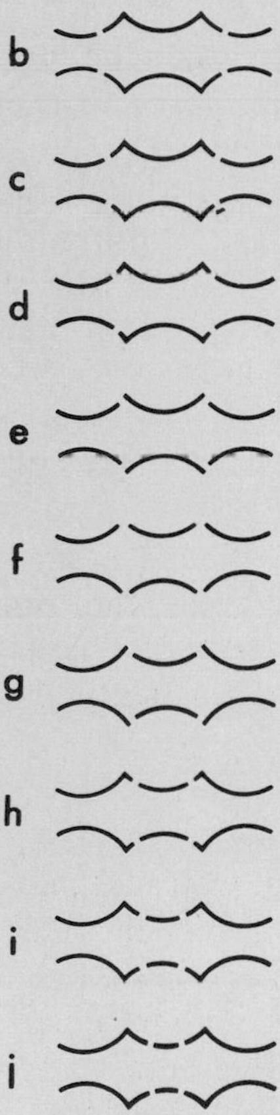

FIGURE 72

		e	d		b[4]	c[4]		
f	(1.3	1.7)	(3.9	5.1	5.3	5.4	5.7)	7.6
	g			h			i	j

	c	b						
d	(1.1	2.0)	(4.0	4.1	[5.7)	6.2	6.3	6.6]
			e	**h**	i	j	**g**	**f**

			d	c	b	g	f	e
h	(1.1	[2.3)	(4.3	4.4]	5.4	5.7	6.3	6.5)
	i	j						

The results are similar to those of Experiment 70, but now there is one significant inversion. With d as the St, h ranks significantly ahead of g and f. There is also an inversion with h as St, involving b, c, d, against e, f, g. Here, however, the difference in rank-

[4] The difference in rank, and hence the inversion, is not significant, as indicated by the parentheses. In the individual choices, c was ranked ahead of b by 6 of 10 subjects.

ing falls short of being significant at the $p = .05$ level. Since this inversion would be important, it was checked by means of a further experiment using h as the St but giving only d and e as CFs. The result was $h \sim d \nsim e$ for 13 of 15 Os, which by the chi-square test is significant, $p < .01$. These experiments, taken together, show that d and h are more similar to each other than at least one and probably two of the intervening designs e, f, and g, and that probably what is true for h also holds for i, and what holds for d may also hold for c. Summarizing these results, one can say that, phenomenally, a gap at a corner is different in kind rather than only in degree from the same sized gap in the interior of a line. With f as the St, e, f, and g are more similar to each other than to any of the designs which have the gaps in the interior ($p < .01$). Conversely, with d or h as the St, f, g, and in one instance also e, rank last, and in both cases are significantly ($p < .01$) less similar to the St than the designs with the gap on the same side as the St (b and c for d, i and j for h). So it matters greatly whether a one-step change goes from h to i (little difference) or from h to g (significant difference), whether a one-step change goes from d to c (little difference) or from d to e (significant difference).

The same principle is embodied in Figure 73. In the first experiment 15 Os were given 73c as the St. The mean rankings were

	b	a			
c	1.3	(2.6	3.3	3.3)	4.5
			d	f	e

Here f ranks ahead of e (for 12 of 15 Os, $p < .05$), and b significantly outranks d (for 14 of 15 Os, $p < .01$) even though they are both one step removed from c; d, only one step from c, is about equal in rank with f, three steps away. Again, these results are related to the singular position of the gaps in d and e.

The control experiment, with still another 15 Os, using d as the St, gave

		c		b	a
d	(1.5	2.0)	3.3	[3.7)	4.5]
	e		f		

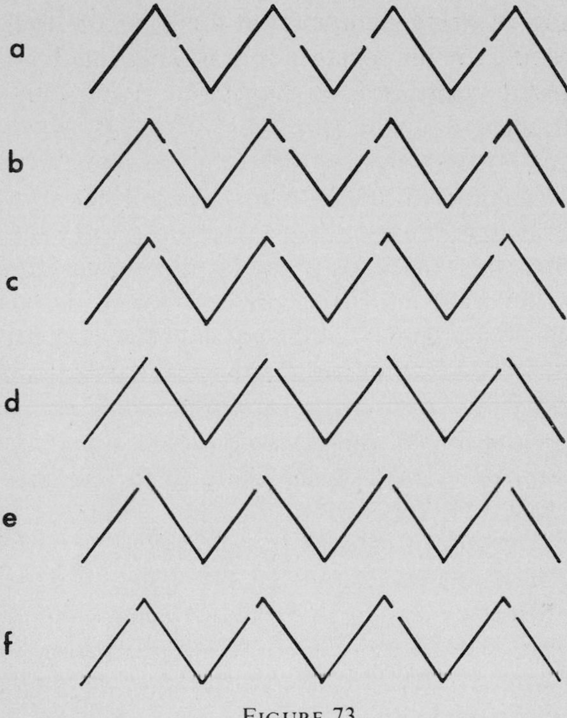

FIGURE 73

In other words, with the gaps in the St at the ends of the lines, no reversals occur.

When there is a reversal in the rankings, they can no longer be represented as points on a straight line. They form a two-dimensional array, as in Figure 74. This suggests that *phenomenally*

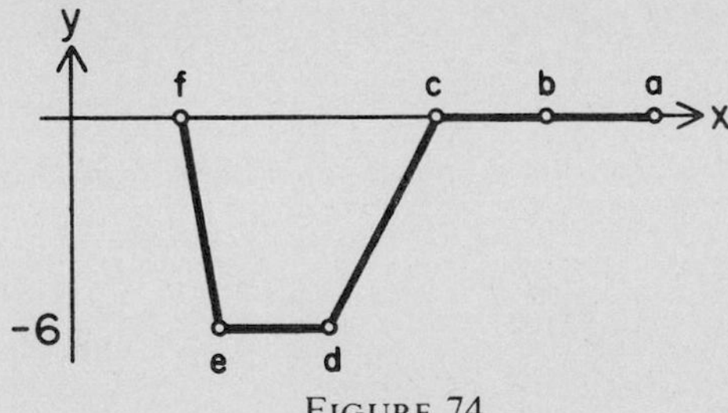

FIGURE 74

there is more than one parameter being varied. The distances between the six points are so chosen that they reflect the rank order in both experiments with Figure 73.

The change along the x-axis corresponds to the geometric change of the parameter. The other dimension, along y, seems to be a two-valued rather than a continuous variable. It indicates whether the gap is *within a curve* (y = 0) or *at a corner,* as in d and e. Figure 74 is based on only two of the six possible rankings and was arrived at by trial and error rather than by the more powerful computer methods available for more extensive data (see, e.g., Kruskal, 1964). I believe that more detailed analysis of more extensive data would reveal an additional dimension which might be called "sidedness," also two-valued, which separates the designs into those with gaps on the *same* side of the corner as the St from designs with gaps on the opposite side.

It might be mentioned here that no O was used for more than one experiment of any one type. Thus Experiments 70, 72, and 73 required 90 Os. Each O was of course given additional tasks at the same session, but with unrelated designs.

59. LINEAR SMOOTHNESS AS A SINGULAR QUALITY: EXPERIMENT 75

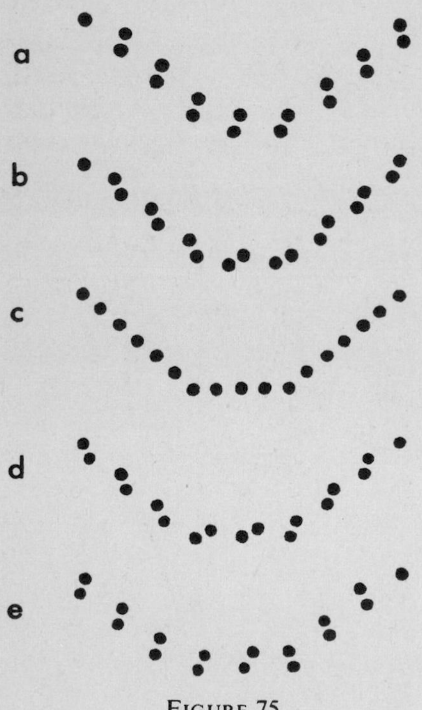

FIGURE 75

One last example, based on still another kind of singularity. The variation in Figure 75 consists in shifting every other dot in a direction forming an angle with the main direction of the entire line. As the dots are shifted from a to b they come closer to the main direction, at c they fall in line with it, at d and e they deviate from it on the other side. The deviation is largest in a and e, less in b and d. In neither pair are the figures mirror images of one another.

With e as the St, the rank order is (for 12 Os)

	a	d	b	c
e	(1.3	1.9)	2.75	4

The geometrically most different CF, a, is the most similar to e. Both a and b are more similar to e than is c, even though in c the dots are shifted less.

With b as the St, the rank order is (for 12 Os)

```
            a
b   (1.4   1.8)   2.9   3.8
            d      e     c
```

and with c as the St (10 Os)

```
           b            a
c   (1.9   2.2   2.6   3.3)
     d            e
```

The results show that the phenomenal differences among the designs are based on the deviation from smooth linearity, as in c, and only very slightly on the direction in which the dots themselves actually deviate. Thus a and e are phenomenally nearly equivalent, though geometrically they are farthest apart. Likewise b and d are nearly equivalent and c is in a class by itself, with zero deviation from "smoothness." The results can be diagramed as in Figure 76 if the order of a and d in Experiment 75b is reversed. This seems permissible since the two rankings do not differ significantly. Figure 76 then also predicts the rankings a-e, b, d, c, and d-b, e, a, c. This prediction was confirmed experimentally (15 Os each):

```
a   (1.5   [1.9)   2.6]   4
      e      b      d     c
```

and

```
      b             a     c
d   (1.4   [2.1)   2.8]   3.7
             e
```

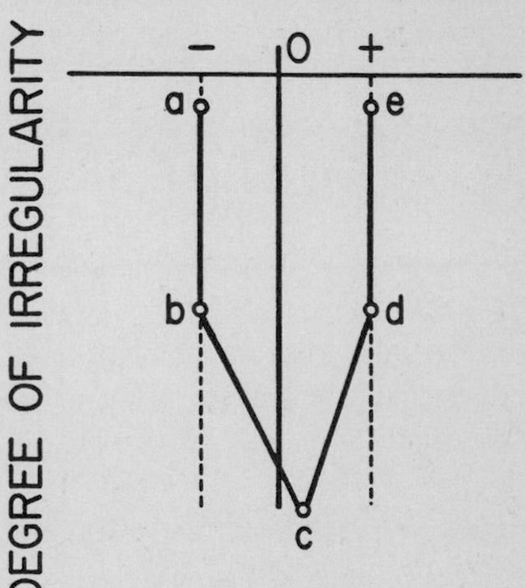

FIGURE 76

60. MONOTONICITY AND REVERSALS

If one parameter is varied, it might be expected that the perceived design will vary in one single respect, with regard to a single attribute, in one dimension, as in Experiment 65. If two independent parameters are varied, the phenomenal form should vary in two dimensions, a situation first investigated by Attneave (1950). But in most of the experiments presented in this chapter monotonic variation of a single parameter led to strikingly different results. The phenomenal change was monotonic except in the small region of singular values of the parameter. There the appearance changed abruptly and qualitatively.

This kind of relation between stimulus variation and phenomenal variation has never been envisioned in psychological theory. The first approach in modern times, the Weber-Fechner law, proposed a logarithmic relation. That law has since been modified and embellished but it has always been taken for granted that the relation should be monotonic, that is, an increase in one should lead to an increase in the other, or at least *not* to a decrease. But in the examples presented in this chapter as well as in many previous ones, monotonic variation of a parameter at first decreases similarity, and then further variation in the same direction increases it again, so that, for instance, in Figure 75, a $\sim$ e $\nsim$ c.

In trying to put these findings in perspective one might say, with Hegel, that quantitative changes eventually become qualitative ones. But this is not very illuminating; moreover, it fails to account for the fact that, in the present experiments, monotonic relations hold again when the narrow region of singularity has been left behind, e.g., in Figure 75, a $\sim$ b $\nsim$ d or b $\sim$ d $\nsim$ e.

61. THE CONCEPT OF SIMILARITY SPACE

A better way to conceptualize these results makes use of the notion of a space, specifically a metric space, as is implied in the representation of the rankings in diagrams like Figure 76 in a "similarity space." The interesting properties of such spaces will not be reviewed in detail. Important aspects of the problem have been presented by Attneave (1950) and Landahl (1945), who were concerned particularly with questions of metric, and by Shepard (1963, 1964), Kruskal (1964), and Torgerson (1965). These references also encompass fairly well the extent and direction which research on similarity has taken since the preceding chapters were published in 1936.

In terms of similarity space, the present experiments show that a one-dimensional variation of a stimulus parameter may induce multidimensional variations in similarity space. The transitions into additional dimensions occur as the parameter passes through particular *singular* values: gap at the corners in Experiments 70, 72, 73, symmetry in 68, parallel course in 67, circularity (convexity) in 69, and smooth linearity in 75. This is the situation mentioned in section 38. On both sides of a singular value similarity space is a one-dimensional, straight line, as in Figure 74, where a, b, c, and f are on a straight line, or in Figure 76, where a-b and d-e are straight lines.

62. DIMENSIONALITY OF SIMILARITY SPACE

Mathematically, additional dimensions are compatible with *any* data, since any N points can be accommodated in N-1 or more dimensions. However, additional dimensions are not necessarily psychologically meaningful. There is such a thing as a psychologically realized or "activated" dimension of change. For example, if Figure 75c alone is presented, a sideways shift of every other dot, as in 75a, b, d, and e, is not phenomenally envisioned, nor activated, any more than is an infinite variety of other possible changes, say, change in diameter of every third dot, or making every other dot square.

An example of conceptual similarity might illustrate this point better. The concept of farm animal extends in one dimension, say, from chicken to pig to cow to horse, and in another, orthogonal, direction from newborn to young to half-grown to fully grown animal. Add to this two-dimensional manifold a pony; it might be fitted in with half-grown horses. But given enough ponies of diverse ages the need for a third dimension, which might be named "variety of horse," becomes evident, and similarly for different varieties of the other farm animals. The number of dimensions is potentially infinite. Which ones are activated—psychologically envisioned—depends on the given manifold which, in the case of concepts, has been called "the universe of discourse," and in the case of objects "the inferred total set" (Garner, 1966). These considerations are of relevance for recall (Whitman and Garner, 1962; Garner and Whitman, 1965) and recognition

(Goldmeier, in preparation) as well as for perception. *In perception there seems to be a tendency to structuring in terms of the minimum possible number of dimensions.* Goodness of gestalt is then a matter of low dimensionality of the space of reference (Garner and Clement, 1963).

63. TOPOLOGY OF SIMILARITY SPACE

Torgerson (1965, pp. 385–386) has called attention to the peculiarity of similarity space that it sometimes is not filled up or that some dimensions are capable of only a few, discrete, values. Many of our examples are of this type. In Figure 76 the ordinate corresponds to a phenomenal dimension of "roughness" or irregularity. This quality certainly ends at c, which is as regular in this respect as is possible. The space beyond c is empty. The abscissa is even more pathological. It seems capable of only three values which give the "sign" of the irregularity: none (0), right (+), or left (–). The two-dimensional space is then reduced to, at most, a U-shaped line. Similarly, the similarity space pictured in Figure 74 is confined to the x-axis except for the region from c to f, where it extends into the y-dimension. This means that the number of dimensions can vary in different regions of the space.

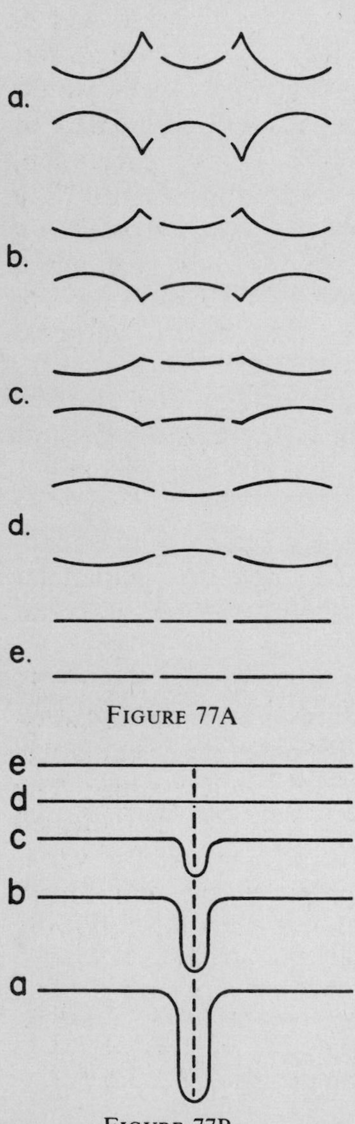

FIGURE 77A

FIGURE 77B

Consider again Figure 72: let each of these patterns vary along a second new parameter, as in Figure 77A, where a new variation is applied to 72h, which is the same as 77b. As the corners become more and more effaced, the dimension "gap within the lines" versus "gap at the corners" loses its geometrical basis. When the variation reaches 77d, there are no

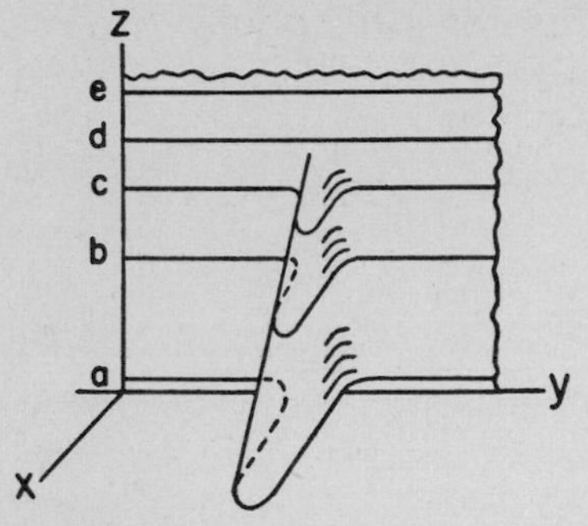

FIGURE 78

x: Gap at corner versus gap in interior.
y: Distance along the lines.
z: Sharpness of corners.

longer any corners to separate the three lines, and the variation of the gaps becomes one-dimensional. The curved similarity space becomes more and more a flat space, as diagramed in Figure 77B. I have not actually repeated Experiment 72h with a series like 77a, another like 77c, and one like 77d and e, as would be necessary to map out this space completely, but I would predict the results represented in Figure 77B. Similarity space, then, would be as shown in Figure 78, a curved surface in three-dimensional space which *flattens into a two-dimensional plane* from d on up. The curves a, b, c, d, and e in Figure 78, which are shown separately in 77B, correspond to the series a, b, c, d, e in Figure 77A with decreasing sharpness of the corners.

64. TWO-PARAMETER VARIATION WITH ONE-DIMENSIONAL SIMILARITY SPACE: EXPERIMENT 79

In the experiments described in this chapter, variation of one geometric parameter gave rise to phenomenal variation in several dimensions.

In the following experiment, Figure 79 a-h, *two* parameters are varied independently. Each of the designs consists of the same five bars alternated with triangular shapes. The triangles are designated by size, as indicated in Figure 79d, as 9, 7, 5, 3, and 1. The variation involves only the second and fourth triangular shape according to the following key:

design	a	b	c	d	e	f	g	h
size of second triangle	7	3	1	7	5	1	7	3
size of fourth triangle	1	7	7	3	3	5	5	3

FIGURE 79

In this group the letters are merely labels;

their alphabetical sequence is not related to the values of the parameters. The eight designs were arbitrarily chosen out of the 16 possible combinations of 1, 3, 5, 7, in pairs of two. Of these, d is the most regular, having the combination 7–3, so that the triangular shapes decrease regularly in size 9–7–5–3–1. On the other hand, b, with 3–7, is the reverse of d: 9–3–5–7–1: the size of the shapes first decreases, then increases, and then decreases again. Three experiments, using 15 Os each, were performed in the same manner as Experiment 65, with designs b, d, and e as the Sts; the resulting rank orders were:

		h		e	g	d	a
b	(2.0	2.9	[3.1	3.7)	(4.6]	[5.4)	6.6]
	c*		f*				
			a				
d	(1.7	2.4	[2.7)	3.7]	(5.1	[5.7)	6.7]
	e*	g*		h	b	f	c
	d*	g*	a				
e	(1.9	2.4	3.1	3.3)	(5.2	[5.3)	6.7]
				h	b	f	c

(* Indicates inversions by comparison with the sequence a, d, g, e, h, b, f, c; see p. 124.)

Figure 80A displays the eight designs as an array according to

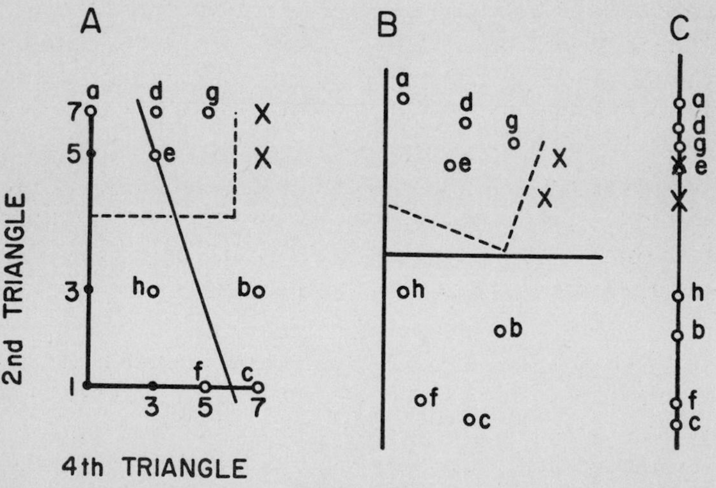

FIGURE 80

The broken lines in A and B separate the region of "monotonic" designs, above, from those with "reversals," below and on the right.

the size of the second and fourth triangles. The scale of triangle sizes is irregular, and it is different along the two coordinate axes. By means of this distortion it was possible to make the distances between the representative points reflect the differences in rank. It is a two-dimensional similarity space, in keeping with the fact that two independent parameters were varied. But phenomenally neither of the two parameters appears to be realized or activated. Inspection of the display itself shows that the points are roughly disposed along a line running through the array on a slant, as drawn in Figure 80A. Figure 80B shows the same group of points rotated, so that the slanted line falls into the vertical. Now it is possible to give a psychological interpretation to the ordinate dimension. The four designs in the upper cluster, a, d, g, e, are *monotonic*, in the sense that the triangular shapes never increase in size from left to right. This gives them a degree of regularity and conformity with the uniformly decreasing pattern of the bars. In this respect d is the most regular, with triangles 9–7–5–3–1. In the other three designs two adjoining triangles are of equal size, e.g., 9–5–5–3–1 in design e.

In the other group, all the designs contain one or two reversals in the sequence of sizes of the triangles: 9–**3**–5–**7**–1 in b, 9–**1**–5–**7**–1 in c, 9–**3**–5–3–1 in h, and 9–**1**–5–5–1 in f. In this respect there is an element of irregularity which clashes with the regularity of the decrease in the length of the bars. The presence or absence of this "clash" makes for less or more *internal consistency,* and in that sense for a "worse" or a "better" figure. Design d would then be singled out as the "best" in this respect, b, with 9–3–5–7–1, two reversals, as bad, and c, with 9–1–5–7–1, also two reversals, as the worst pattern. One result of the three experiments is, then: monotonic designs are more similar to one another than to those containing reversals, and designs containing reversals are more similar to one another than to monotonic ones.

In Figure 80A the region of monotonic designs is indicated by a broken line. It shows that two possible members of the reversed set, marked by ×'s, would lie rather high on the monotonic-reversal axis if they had been included in the series of designs, and if Figures 80A and B correctly predict their similarity relations. Also, there is no obvious phenomenal meaning to the dimension of the abscissa of 80B in this representation. This leaves only one meaningful dimension in Figure 80B, with the remaining dimension unanalyzed. Further analysis might be possible with more extensive data. On the other hand, the one dimension obtained does reflect all the significant and most of the nonsignificant differences in rank. Reading from the top downward, the sequence is a, d, g, e, h, b, f, c, as shown in Figure 80C. Comparison with the actual rankings obtained (p. 122) shows only minor discrepancies (indicated by asterisks) in each of the three rankings, none of them involving significant differences. The final result is, then, a one-dimensional similarity space, 80C, which accounts quite well for the two-dimensional variation in stimulus space. Phenomenally, neither of the two stimulus parameters is realized separately. Their variation gives rise to change of a single whole quality which dominates the similarity relations. It involves the regularity, or better, the "consistency" between the regularly decreasing pattern of the bars and the degree of deviation from regular decrease of the triangles. Slight deviations, with preservation of monotonicity, seem to be well tolerated, as suggested by the close clustering of the monotonic patterns a, d, g, e. But if this whole quality is impaired, no *one* "good" structuring is available; the nonsingular designs are further apart from one another as well as from the most regular design, d. The singularity of the designs diminishes by steps. Design 79d is completely regular; bars and triangles decrease together. Next are the three monotonic designs a, e, and g. Then comes h, with one reversal but an otherwise regular decrease as in d; and finally b, f, and c, without regular decreases at all and one reversal (f) or two (b, c). This analysis of singularity alone thus accounts for all significant differences in rank in 80C and for the three clusters of (1) monotonic designs (a, d, e, g), (2) one with one reversal but regularly decreasing otherwise (h), and (3) those with reversals without regularity of this kind (b, f, c).

65. SYNOPSIS OF SIMILARITY SPACE

The picture of similarity space that emerges here is characterized by the following features.

1. Monotonic variation of one geometric property in a series of related designs does not necessarily evoke, phenomenally, corresponding graded variations of similarity along a single dimen-

sion.[5] Many of the examples given in this chapter were so constructed that a one-dimensional stimulus change induced a two-dimensional similarity space, but more than two dimensions could result (section 58).

2. The scale, as tested by the distances along one axis, is not necessarily proportional, or related by a simple transformation, to the geometric change along that axis. In fact, it is quite arbitrary how the geometric change is measured, for instance as in Figure 66A or 66B or in still other ways.

3. The following point is rather mathematical and will not be treated in detail (see Attneave, 1950; Kruskal, 1964). The dimensions which do arise determine particular axes in similarity space. In general it is not possible to rotate the space and refer it to rotated axes, as can be done without restriction in Euclidean spaces. This is an important concern of Attneave's (1950) paper and is further discussed by Torgerson (1965) and others. The present results contribute little to this question and to the related problem of what metric is appropriate to similarity space, whether the Euclidean or, for example, the "city block" metric favored by Attneave, but they certainly suggest that the axes of similarity space are fixed. Nevertheless, it was possible, and certainly very convenient, to employ a Euclidean distance function in the diagrams presented in this chapter.

4. Besides not being Euclidean, similarity space is unusual in another way: it is far from continuous (section 63). It may consist of mere unconnected lines, or even isolated points, as in the case of Morse code, where one dimension turns out to be the number of elements in a symbol (Shepard, 1963). This is inherently discontinuous, capable of only five discrete values. Figure 74 is another example. The y-dimension reflects the position of the gap in relation to the corner. It has only two values, "at the corner" or "not at the corner." Since there is no other possibility, the similarity space between the lines $y = 0$ and $y = -6$ is empty. Furthermore, the line $y = -6$ extends only from e to d. Beyond these points the gap cannot be at the corners. Thus Figure 74

[5] This fact intruded itself unexpectedly into an experiment of Attneave's (1950, p. 525) and was also observed by Torgerson (1965, p. 386); in both cases the cause was symmetry, as in Experiment 68. But symmetry is only one of an infinity of singular whole qualities which can bring this about.

should be redrawn as in Figure 81, with three disconnected lines. The line e-d corresponds to those designs in which the gaps straddle the corners. Torgerson (1965) found similar U-shaped

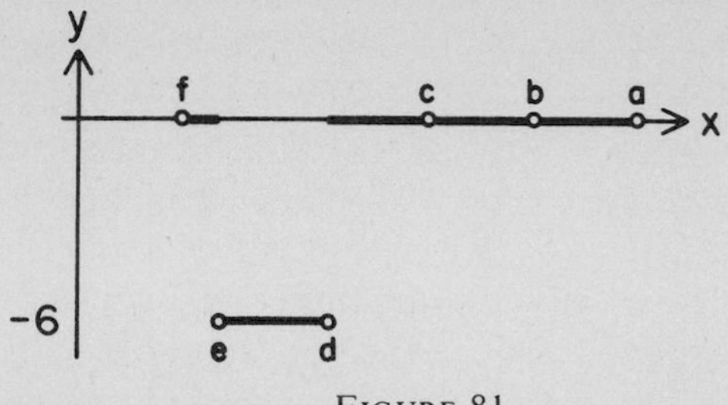

FIGURE 81

similarity spaces. A further example of a U-shape is Figure 76. Other, equally unconventional or pathological topologies will undoubtedly be discovered.

5. In some regions, a similarity space may degenerate into a space of lower dimensionality, as shown in Figure 80; or, looking at the matter from the opposite point of view, the removal of a degeneracy may add a new dimension in the course of certain variations.

66. A PHYSICAL ANALOGY: SINGULARITY AND REVERSALS

The notion of a similarity space affords a concise representation of the similarity relations between patterns. But it is purely descriptive. It is silent about the reason for similarity. Particularly in need of clarification is the reason for the inversions demonstrated in this chapter with what is geometrically a monotonic variation of a parameter. Before turning to this problem it might be well to realize that such situations also occur in other fields, especially in physics. One instance is furnished by a water faucet with a loose washer. As the faucet is opened wider the sound of the flowing water becomes louder. At a certain point, however, the sound changes to a chatter or a high-pitched whistle. Opening the faucet still further stops the chatter or whistle but lets the sound of flow increase still further. Figure 81 may be considered a diagram of this sequence. The sound increases from a to f; the whistle is present from d to e. Opening the faucet is a monotonic change. The monotonic increase in sound, however, is interrupted by a noise which occurs only in a limited subregion of the total range of variation. Another example, this one from optics, is found in the nonreflective coating of optical surfaces. Its thickness is usually chosen to equal a quarter wavelength of green light. As the wavelength of the incident light varies, it is at first partially reflected; as the wavelength gets shorter, reflection decreases and goes to nearly zero at the wavelength of green light, to increase again for still shorter wavelengths. A similar situation, in the atomic domain, is the Ramsauer effect. Here atoms are transparent for matter waves of a certain wavelength but opaque for wavelengths which are either longer or shorter.

One final example from mechanics. Assume a heavy mass at rest (M in Figure 82) and smaller masses flying by it, all with the

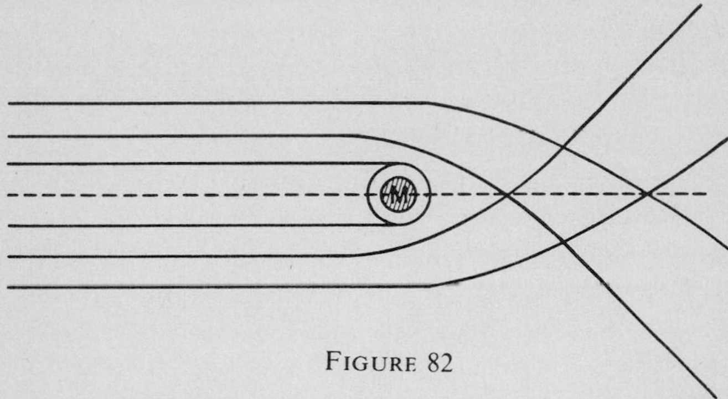

FIGURE 82

same velocity but at varying distances of closest approach to M, as measured by an impact parameter p. As the impact parameter decreases, the smaller masses are deflected more and more strongly. Finally, below a certain absolute value of p they are captured and remain in orbit around M. As p goes through its minimum and then increases again on the other side of M the trajectories again become hyperbolic deflections, as before.

These analogies should not suggest any brain mechanism suitable to explain the peculiarities of similarity. They should merely assist in elaborating the formal, structural characteristics which become operative within different regions within the range of variation of a parameter. In the physical cases the events are of one kind on both sides of a "critical" range and of another kind within the range. Typically, (1) the "critical" range is narrow. (2) Often the transition is quite sharp, as when a configuration of fissionable material attains "critical mass." (3) The interaction within the critical range is different in kind, rather than merely in degree, from the interaction outside that range. (4) Within the critical range small changes of the parameter have large effects; outside of it the process is quite insensitive to even large changes of the parameter. These are the same observations which were made at the end of section 34 in regard to singular values of a parameter and which were reported by Wertheimer (1923, p. 319) as operative in visual organization. In physics the phenomena are due to regions of resonances, of scattering potentials, or to bound states, and expressed in some cases as U-shaped curves, as potential wells, in other instances as Dirac delta functions. In psychology they are linked to regions of *Prägnanz* or singularity.

If a singularity occurs within the range of variation it may merely result in larger phenomenal effects, greater sensitivity to relatively smaller changes, as in Experiments 65 and 79 where the singular designs are clustered together. If the singularity is sharper, confined to a narrow range, more like a delta function in physics, it gives rise to an additional dimension in similarity space as in Experiment 67.

The design with the singularity is more stable, is a "better" figure, becomes the standard of reference for the other designs. The nonsingular designs are perceived *in terms of,* as *deviating from,* the singular one. Thus, in the series of Figure 72 the designs e, f, g, particulary f, are the standard, are "better" designs than the others. Designs 72d and h are relatively similar to each other because they deviate from the standard to the same extent, although in opposite directions. The inversion, as we have seen, leads to the additional dimension.

Rank orders in a series of related designs bring out the *asymmetry* between singular and nonsingular properties, between better and less good designs (see also Handel and Garner, 1966). With the singular pattern as the St, the ranking parallels the change in parameter–there are no reversals; with nonsingular patterns reversals do occur. A good example is Experiment 75, diagramed in Figure 76. The "best" design, c, with the singular value of the parameter, is the only one without reversals; the nonsingular patterns, a, b, d, and e, all have reversals. This asymmetry provides independent evidence for the distinctive role played by singularities.

SUMMARY

Similarity cannot always be defined as partial identity (Hypothesis I), nor as identity of relations or proportions (Hypothesis II). There are even cases (Chapter 3) where an exactly proportional variant of a design appears less similar to it than does a disproportional variant. In these cases only what we have called "the form" is varied proportionally while "the material" of the design is kept unchanged (Rule 1 of Chapter 3). The phenomenal separation into material and form occurs in such a way that relatively small and repetitive features are relegated to the phenomenal role of material (Rule 2 of Chapter 3).

With changes in the phenomenal *interrelationship of the parts* and in the phenomenal *structure* in general, similarity is the greater the more faithfully these phenomenal qualities are preserved (Chapter 4). Of particular importance for the similarity of a variant is the preservation of the phenomenal *function of the parts within the whole.*

In the case of distortions, those attributes which have *singular (prägnant)* values are found to be particularly sensitive to change (Chapter 5). In general, it may be said that similarity consists in agreement with respect to the *singular* whole qualities which determine the phenomenal appearance of a figure.

The similarity relations seen with variation of orientation in space (Chapter 6) and with variation of a single geometric parameter (Chapter 7) can also be understood as based on agreement of the designs with respect to these phenomenal qualities.

BIBLIOGRAPHY

Asch, S. E., Ceraso, J., & Heimer, W. (1960), Perceptual Conditions of Association. *Psychol. Monogr.*, 74(3, Whole No. 490).

Attneave, F. (1950), Dimensions of Similarity. *Amer. J. Psychol.*, 63: 516–556.

——— (1954), Some Informational Aspects of Visual Perception. *Psychol. Rev.*, 61: 183–193.

Biemüller, W. (1930), Wiedergabe der Gliederanzahl and Gliederungsform optischer Komplexe. *Neue Psychol. Stud.*, 4: 161–285.

Clauberg, –., & Dubislav, –. (1923), *Wörterbuch der Philosophie.*

Cornelius, H. (1897), *Psychologie als Erfahrungswissenschaft.* Leipzig: Teubner.

Ebbinghaus, H. (1911), *Grundzüge der Psychologie.* Leipzig: Veit.

Ehrenfels, C. von (1890), *Vierteljahresschrift für wissenschaftliche Philosophie,* Vol. 14.

Eisler, R. (1927), *Wörterbuch der philosophischen Begriffe.* Berlin: Mittler.

Garner, W. R. (1966), To Perceive Is to Know. *Amer. Psychol.*, 21: 11–19.

——— & Clement, D. E. (1963), Goodness of Pattern and Pattern Uncertainty. *J. Verbal Learn. Verbal Behav.*, 2: 446–452.

——— & Whitman, J. R. (1965), Form and Amount of Internal Structure as Factors in Free-Recall Learning of Nonsense Words. *J. Verbal Learn. Verbal Behav.*, 4: 257–266.

Goldmeier, E. (1936), Über Ähnlichkeit bei gesehenen Figuren. *Psychol. Forsch.*, 21: 146–208.

——— (in preparation), The Fate of the Memory Trace.

Handel, S., & Garner, W. R. (1966), The Structure of Visual Pattern Associates and Pattern Goodness. *Percept. Psychophys.*, 1: 33–38.

Hochberg, J., & McAlister, E. (1953), A Quantitative Approach to Figural "Goodness." *J. Exper. Psychol.*, 46: 361–364.

Höffding, H. (1901), *Psychologie.* Leipzig.

Katti, S. K. (1968), Exact Distribution of Chi-Square Test in a One-Way Table. Paper presented at the August meeting of the American Statistical Association, Pittsburgh, Penna.

Köhler, W. (1913), On Unnoticed Sensations and Errors of Judgment. *The Selected Papers of Wolfgang Köhler,* ed. M. Henle. New York: Liveright, 1971.

Kopfermann, H. (1930), Psychologische Untersuchungen über die Wirkung zweidimensionaler Darstellungen Körperlicher Gebilde. *Psychol. Forsch.*, 13: 293–365.

Kruskal, J. B. (1964), Multidimensional Scaling by Optimizing Goodness of Fit to a Nonmetric Hypothesis. *Psychometrika,* 29: 1–27.

Lanczos, C. (1966), *The Variational Principles of Mechanics.* Toronto: University of Toronto Press.

Landahl, H. D. (1945), Neural Mechanism fo· the Concepts of Difference and Similarity. *Bull. Math. Biophysics,* 7: 83–88.

Lewin, K. (1923), Über die Umkehrung der Raumlage auf dem Kopf stehender Worte und Figuren in der Wahrnehmung. *Psychol. Forsch.*, 4: 210–261.

Mach, E. (1902), Die Ähnlichkeit und die Analogie als Leitmotiv der Forschung. *Annal. Naturphilos.*, 1: 5–14.

——— (1906), *The Analysis of Sensations,* tr. 5th ed. New York: Dover, 1959.
Matthaei, R. (1929), Das Gestaltproblem. *Erg. Physiol.,* 29: 1–82.
Metzger, W. (1934), Tiefenerscheinungen in optischen Bewegungsfeldern. *Psychol. Forsch.,* 20: 195–260.
Miller, G. A. (1956), The Magical Number Seven, plus or minus Two. *Psychol. Rev.,* 63: 81–97.
Münsterberg, H. (1900), *Grundzüge der Psychologie,* Vol. 1. Leipzig: Barth.
Oppenheimer, E. (1934), Optische Versuche über Ruhe und Bewegung. *Psychol. Forsch.,* 20: 1–46.
Rock, I. (1966), *The Nature of Perceptual Adaptation.* New York: Basic Books.
——— & Kaufman, L. (1962), The Moon Illusion. Part II. *Science,* 136: 1023–1031.
——— & Leaman, R. (1963), An Experimental Analysis of Visual Symmetry. *Acta Psychol.,* 21: 171–183.
Rubin, E. (1921), *Visuell wahrgenommene Figuren.* Copenhagen: Gyldendalska.
Rupp, H. (1914), *Berichte des VI. Kongress für experimentelle Psychologie.*
Sachs, H. (1897), *Die Entstehung der Raumvorstellung aus Sinnesempfindungen.* Breslau: Schlettersche Buchh.
Schneider, C. (1932), *Neue Psychol. Stud.,* 4: 585f.
Schumann, F. (1900), Beiträge zur Analyse der Gesichtswahrnehmungen. *Z. Psychol.,* 23: 1–32.
Schur, E. (1925), Mondtäuschung und Sehgrössenkonstanz. *Psychol. Forsch.,* 7: 44–81.
Shepard, R. N. (1963), Analysis of Proximities as a Technique for the Study of Information Processing in Man. *Hum. Factors,* 5: 33–48.
——— (1964), Attention and the Metric Structure of the Stimulus Space. *J. Mathemat. Psychol.,* 1: 54–87.
Spearman, C. (1925), The New Psychology of Shape. *Brit. J. Psychol.,* 15: 211–225.
Stratton, G. M. (1902), Eye-Movements and the Aesthetics of Visual Form. *Philos. Stud.,* 20: 336–359.
Stumpf, C. (1883), *Tonpsychologie,* Vol. 1. Leipzig: Hirzel.
Ternus, J. (1926), Experimentelle Untersuchung über phänomenale Identität. *Psychol. Forsch.,* 7: 81–136. Abridged translation, The Problem of Phenomenal Identity. In *A Source Book of Gestalt Psychology,* Selection 11, ed. W. D. Ellis. New York: Humanities Press, 1950, pp. 149–160.
Torgerson, W. S. (1965), Multidimensional Scaling of Similarity. *Psychometrika,* 30: 379–393.
Wertheimer, M. (1912a), Über das Denken der Naturvölker, Zahlen und Zahlgebilde. *Z. Psychol.,* 60: 321–378. Abridged translation, Numbers and Numerical Concepts in Primitive Peoples. In *A Source Book of Gestalt Psychology,* Selection 22, ed. W. D. Ellis. New York: Humanities Press, 1950, pp. 265–273.
——— (1912b), Experimental Studies on the Seeing of Motion. In *Classics in Modern Psychology,* ed. T. Shipley. New York: Philosophical Library, 1961, pp. 1032–1089.
——— (1923), Untersuchungen zur Lehre von der Gestalt. *Psychol. Forsch.,* 4: 301–350. Abridged translation, Laws of Organization in Perceptual Forms. In *A Source Book of Gestalt Psychology,* Selection 5, ed. W. D. Ellis. New York: Humanities Press, 1950, pp. 71–88.
——— (1933), Zu dem Problem der Unterscheidung von Einzelinhalt und Teil. *Z. Psychol.,* 129: 353–357.
Whitman, J. R., & Garner, W. R. (1962), Free Recall Learning of Visual Figures as a Function of Form of Internal Structure. *J. Exper Psychol.,* 64: 558–564.
Yourgrau, W., & Mandelstam, S. (1968), *Variational Principles in Dynamics and Quantum Theory.* Philadelphia: Saunders.

INDEX

ABOUT THE AUTHORS

ERICH GOLDMEIER studied psychology under Max Wertheimer at the University of Frankfurt and received his Ph.D. in psychology in 1936. He received his M.D. from the same University in 1938. Since his emigration to the United States in the same year, he has practiced medicine, first in general practice and since 1955 with the Veterans Administration. In 1962 he received a Master's Degree in Physics from Johns Hopkins University. In 1966 he joined the psychiatric staff of the V.A. Hospital, Montrose, New York. In 1970 he was appointed Adjunct Professor of Psychology at the Institute for Cognitive Studies of Rutgers University at Newark, N.J.

IRVIN ROCK received his Ph.D from the Graduate Faculty of the New School for Social Research in 1952. He was a member of the Graduate Faculty until going to Yeshiva University in 1959. Since 1967 he has been professor of Psychology at the Institute for Cognitive Studies, Rutgers University, Newark. His field of major interest is perception; he has also published in the areas of learning and memory.